Medieval Africa

Discovering Lost Stories from Africa's Middle Ages

Free Bonus from Captivating History
(Available for a Limited time)

Hi History Lovers!

Now you have a chance to join our exclusive history list so you can get your first history ebook for free as well as discounts and a potential to get more history books for free!

Simply visit the link below to join.

Or, Scan the QR code!

<u>captivatinghistory.com/ebook</u>

Also, make sure to follow us on Facebook, X, and YouTube by searching for Captivating History.

Table of Contents

Introduction

If you ask most people what they know about Africa in the Middle Ages, many will not have much to say. Perhaps they imagine dry deserts with mountains of sand or endless forests that different kinds of exotic animals call home. Some may even think of ancient Egypt, which thrived on the continent long before the Middle Ages, or maybe European explorers, who arrived much later. Only a few picture kings sitting on ivory thrones, lively markets full of gold, old universities where scholars debated science and faith, or warrior queens leading armies against invaders.

The myth that Africa lacked civilization or complexity during the medieval era has to be abandoned. Not only is that idea outdated, but it is deeply misleading. While Romanesque and Gothic cathedrals rose in Europe and many dynasties emerged and fell in China, Africa was also thriving. From the gold-laden courts of Mali to the heavily walled cities of the Hausa states and from the wealthy coastal cities of Swahili to the busyness of Timbuktu, where scholars from all over the world converged, Africa clearly had its hands full shaping its own world on its own terms.

Especially during the medieval period, Africa was the envy of many colossal powers of the world. Unfortunately, today, its story is rarely told from beginning to end. Despite the importance of the African kingdoms at the time, such as the Songhai Empire, the Mali Empire, Great Zimbabwe, and the Ajuran Sultanate, their stories are typically reduced to footnotes. The names of African rulers, warriors, and scholars appeared only a few times—if any—in schoolbooks. Not only are their cities left forgotten, but their achievements also rarely get the attention they deserve. Even the maps of medieval trade routes often ignore the many networks that once stretched across the Sahara.

This book is here to change our views on African history. It continues the journey that began in our previous volume, *Ancient Africa: Discovering Lost Stories from Africa's Early Civilizations*, in which we traveled thousands of years in the past when the early roots of African civilization first emerged. That book gave insights into the early kingdoms on the continent and their culture, as well as various innovations that laid the foundation for what came next. This book picks up the story in the medieval period, an era that gave birth to dozens of powerful kings, queens, and warriors. It was a period filled with thriving trade activities, world-class scholars, impressive architecture, and cities that could rival even those in Europe and Asia.

Here, you will not find textbook lists of dates or long and complicated academic theories. Instead, you will journey through medieval Africa like a story. You will be introduced to the people who built, ruled, resisted, and dreamed. You will experience kingdoms and cities as if they were still around. Indeed, some names may sound unfamiliar at first, but by the last page of the book, they will feel unforgettable.

Chapter 1 – The Hidden Realms of Medieval Ghana

The desert was unrelenting. Each gust kicked up sheets of sand that could sting the skin like needles. Some people's nostrils filled with tiny specks of dust, so much so that it began choking their throats. Yet, this did not stop a certain merchant from continuing his journey. Hailing from Sijilmasa (a booming Saharan trade hub in present-day southeastern Morocco), it was common for merchants like him to see caravans of gold from the mysterious lands of the south entering the city. However, despite the regular flow of these precious metals, only a few knew where the gold came from. To venture south, beyond the safety of familiar paths, was rare and often discouraged.

Our merchant preferred to do what the others did not. He was intrigued by the stories of a mysterious city where gold was very plentiful. Some even said that their kings did not sit on typical thrones but on ones completely made of ivory. Their courtiers were also said to have dusted themselves in powdered gold, making their entire bodies glisten when the sun rose high up in the sky. Indeed, no map marked its precise location, but through stories that spread like wildfire across North Africa, he finally learned the name of the empire. Some referred to it as Wagadu, while others called it Ghana.

When the merchant first announced to his friends that he planned to set foot in the wealthy land of Ghana, he was met with laughter.

"Surely, you are jesting," one of them said.

"You will probably be swallowed by the dunes before you could even reach Aoudaghost," another scoffed.

"Or perhaps robbed blind by raiders in the desert long before you see the smallest speck of gold," another of his friends muttered.

The older merchants did not give their opinion, but their silence and expressions said everything. They had seen too many ambitious men vanish in the desert, dead and forever buried beneath the sand. The journey south was not a piece of cake. Ghana was sandwiched between extremes: the perilous Sahara to the north and the deep forest of unknown spirits and tangled trade routes to the south. The Sahara was seen more as an ocean than land. The desert was endless and unpredictable. Whoever traveled through it would see skeletons of caravans and even humans left in the sands.

Still, the curious merchant went. He was tired of only listening to stories describing Ghana. He wished to see its glorious capital with his own eyes.

And so, the merchant joined a caravan that departed from Sijilmasa to Taghaza (a salt-mining center in present-day northern Mali). Here, the camels were laden with heavy slabs of the white mineral. The merchant and the caravan then pushed south, eventually reaching Aoudaghost (an important southern Saharan trade town in present-day southeastern Mauritania). During the day, the air dried the merchant's lips. The merciless sun caused sweat to drip from his skin. At night, he could hear nothing except the sound of the creak of the saddle and the whisper of wind brushing against the sand.

The merchant also had to endure a sandstorm that swallowed the sky within minutes. He witnessed a few camels collapse from heat and went through a near-death experience when his water ran dangerously low. There were times when he questioned his journey, but before doubt could settle deep in his bones, signs began to appear. His caravan was soon joined by traders with darker skin who spoke in dialects that were unfamiliar to his ears. These traders had kola nuts, elephant tusks, and carved wooden charms.

Trade routes of the western Sahara Desert, c. 1000–1500.[1]

They proceeded along the route until the merchant could finally see Koumbi Saleh, the fabled capital of the Ghana Empire, from afar. Squinting his eyes, the merchant could spot a cluster of sunbaked buildings, some featuring flat rooftops and others crowned by minarets. His eyes widened as he drew closer. All this time, he had heard only stories of the city, but now, he could see with his own eyes the city for what it truly was—a heartbeat in the middle of a desert.

What intrigued the merchant the most was the distinct sections of the grand city. The 11th-century Arab geographer al-Bakri wrote that the capital was made up of two very different parts, both in function and in population. On one side was the commercial city. This was where the merchant could see traders like himself conducting their businesses in an array of tongues. Mosques also adorned this part of the city. The other part of the city was less busy yet far more extravagant. Closed off to outsiders, this was where the king and his court resided.

The rumors he heard back home about Ghana were true; gold was indeed everywhere. Of course, the metal was not scattered carelessly across the streets like the wild tales from the north would suggest. The merchant never saw children tossing nuggets of gold as they played around the city. Not all women adorned themselves in gold; they were more likely to wear beads of copper or shells rather than pure gold. However, golden ornaments were commonly seen on the elites, wealthy merchants, and officials. They wore them as rings, pendants, or small threaded beads.

Trans-Saharan camel caravan carrying salt.[3]

Regardless, the very first time the merchant saw gold changing hands in the open market, he froze. Despite its precious value, gold in Ghana was exchanged almost casually alongside cloth, salt, or ivory. The trade did not come with the pomp or anxiety that he had seen in other places where even a sliver of it demanded armed guards. It was as if gold was their currency.

The merchant remained in the city for quite some time. He was enthralled by the wealth of Ghana and its deep history. He listened to the stories told by the griots (oral historians, storytellers, poets, and musicians in West African cultures) that told of how the kingdom first came to be. According to these oral traditions, it all started with the Soninke people, who built their homes near the Senegal and Niger Rivers.

Over time, the Soninke grew in influence. They were able to organize themselves into powerful clans and, eventually, established a centralized monarchy that controlled key trade routes between the merchants of the north and the gold-producing regions of the south. It was also through stories passed by the griots that the curious merchant finally learned what he had never known back home in Sijilmasa: the gold that had been flowing into his city for years had come from the Bambouk region, a rich goldfield nestled near the Upper Senegal River.

As a giant hub of trans-Saharan commerce, Ghana attracted people from every corner of the world—from Berber traders to Arabic scribes and African artisans. Goods came in from all directions. The empire saw camels carrying salt from Taghaza, fine cloth from Egypt, and exceptional horses from Maghreb, to name a few. However, the more time our curious merchant spent in Koumbi Saleh, the more he realized that what met the eye was only the surface. He came to understand that it was not gold alone that made Ghana thrive. It was also how it was governed and held together by its people.

Al-Bakri, in particular, wrote that at the top of the hierarchy was the Ghana himself. This was a title used to refer to the ruler of the empire. Like many other monarchs, the Ghana possessed both political and spiritual authority, with the people typically seeing their king as semi-divine. At times, the king was also referred to as Kaya Maghan (translated as Lord of the Gold), a title associated with the king's monopoly over the gold trade.

Of course, the Ghana did not rule alone. Al-Bakri provided no detailed names for the king's council. However, he did write that the king was assisted by ministers and officials, including judges and interpreters. It was common for most West African monarchies to operate with the support of a council of elders and religious leaders, so it is safe to assume that the Ghana Empire was governed with the guidance of such a council. Beneath the king and the elders were regional chiefs and local leaders. They held power over their own territories, where they were in charge of collecting taxes, maintaining order, and offering tribute to the royal court.

The merchant also learned that there were things older than the law. During his stay, he heard murmurs that the empire was also protected by mysteries. The people of Ghana told him that their king was far more than just a political leader. Although there is no specific written or physical evidence, oral traditions and anthropological studies have revealed that it was a common belief that the rulers of Ghana (as well as other West African monarchies) possessed some sort of mystical qualities. Some spoke of these kings being protected by ancestral spirits, while others talked about sacred objects that were kept by the royals and hidden from the common people. They believed that these relics— whether stones, staffs, or even carvings—possessed *baraka*, a mysterious spiritual force that had the ability to bless and shield their kingdom.

Interestingly, when the king passed, news of his death was not announced to the public immediately. The people might continue their daily work unaware that their ruler was no longer breathing. Mourning rituals were performed in private by the royal family and officials. This was so that the transition of power could be arranged smoothly without any hassle. It was only after succession was secured and the proper rituals were completed that word of the king's passing would be announced to the public. This delay could range from a few days to even weeks. Once announced, the empire would enter public mourning ceremonies. Royal funerary rites would take place, followed by proclamations of the new ruler's ascension.

Although the king was placed at the top of the hierarchy, the spiritual life in Ghana did not orbit solely around him. The Soninke and other peoples of the empire followed animistic traditions. They believed nature, ancestors, and unseen forces all held power over their lives. Trees were sacred, and rivers could hear their prayers.

Nevertheless, animism was not the only belief system practiced by the people of Ghana. The empire was also influenced by Islam, which likely began to take root in Ghana sometime in the 8th century. By the time our curious merchant stepped into the city of Koumbi Saleh, Islamic influence was already becoming more visible. Mosques dotted the region, and scholars could be seen reciting Arabic verses. However, while Islam was primarily practiced by foreign and local merchants, those in the palace and much of the rural population continued to practice animistic and ancestral traditions. Still, religious syncretism existed. This means individuals combined both Islamic and older spiritual traditions.

At first glimpse, many saw the production and trade of gold as the main reason behind Ghana's success. However, as our merchant lingered longer in the capital city, he came to realize that the people also valued salt. Caravans from Taghaza in the north, just like the one our curious merchant joined, would bring in blocks of salt so precious that they were treated like any other luxury item. Salt can preserve food, cure meat, and replenish the body. It was very important for people living in the hot, humid zones in the south. At times, it was considered more valuable than gold.

Kola nuts also filled the markets. They typically arrived in baskets from the forest belt farther south. These bitter and aromatic nuts have a mildly energizing effect on the body, similar to how caffeine works in coffee or tea. Traders and nobles chewed the nut during negotiations. They were also used in rituals and offered as symbols of respect.

Ivory, as well as gold, was widely used in ornaments. This prized organic material was shipped northward, where it was usually turned into dagger handles, inlaid boxes, or even gifts for caliphs and sultans. Slaves also passed through the empire. They were often traded as part of tribute systems. Their fates varied. While some ended up in North African households, others were forced to serve in distant military garrisons or administrative posts.

The merchant saw the trade of various other items that came from far beyond Ghana's borders. Glass beads came all the way from North Africa, and silk fragments arrived from China. There were also spices and copperware that came from distant coasts. This wide selection of goods made the merchant certain that Ghana did not just control a trade network. He knew the empire was part of a vast, layered system of movement that stretched across continents—the kingdom's reach went far beyond what he had ever imagined. Informal trade corridors threaded through small towns, forest clearings, river bends, and mountain passes, carrying all sorts of goods, legends, stories, and gossip.

The merchant did not only remain behind the safe walls of Koumbi Saleh. After a while, he journeyed outward from the capital, visiting smaller trade outposts. On his travels, he noticed the military strength of the empire. The men were stationed differently compared to the soldiers he usually saw in cities farther north. In contrast to cities like Fez or Kairouan, the soldiers typically had a rather formal and visible presence. They usually wore uniforms complete with emblems. Like many other West African cities, the soldiers and guards of Koumbi Saleh were, at times, indistinguishable from ordinary citizens. They did not always wear formal uniforms, but those observant enough could easily recognize their bearing and quiet vigilance.

Although sources are limited, it is safe to assume that Ghana had its own royal guard of elite military corps since this was a common feature in many West African kingdoms. Scholars suggest that the elite royal guards of the Ghana Empire likely carried iron weapons. After all, Ghana had access to ironworking technology. These elite soldiers were sworn to protect not only the king but also the kingdom itself. The empire must have had regional militias as well. These would have been placed under the command of local chiefs. These forces were in charge of enforcing the king's laws and dealing with smaller threats, such as banditry and border skirmishes. Though varied in composition, they followed a clear chain of command and were supported by Ghana's tax system. This ensured a steady supply of equipment and provisions.

The empire had impressive defensive strategies. Towns located on the empire's edge were fortified not with towering stone walls but with well-positioned barricades and natural defenses. Watch posts were also installed, allowing the garrisons to communicate or signal dangers with drums or horns. Entry into these settlements was monitored. Caravans were often registered.

Our curious merchant then returned to Koumbi Saleh. Throughout his travels, he had seen a kingdom of not just wealth but also order and might. One thing that puzzled him, however, was the absence of the empire's own records.

Interestingly, the Ghana Empire did not develop a known written script of its own. The empire also did not leave behind inscriptions, royal decrees, or even carved monuments like those found in Egypt or Mesopotamia. Most of what we know about the once-flourishing empire came from outside observers like Muslim scholars al-Fazari (8th century), al-Khwarizmi (9th century), and al-Bakri (11th century). The latter wrote the most detailed account of the empire, though he never set foot in Ghana himself. Instead, al-Bakri relied solely on reports from North African merchants, like our curious merchant.

Most of these stories of the empire, including its laws, customs, and history, were not written down on parchment. Instead, they were remembered. They were passed down by griots. Typically trained from a young age, griots were considered the living memory of the Ghana Empire. They could recite genealogies that stretched back centuries, recount the deeds of the many kings of Ghana, and narrate the rise of clans and the turning points of each battle that took place in the region. Their traditions were incredibly detailed and consistent, even across generations. Outsiders might have seen them as mere entertainers who spoke of legends and stories, but to the people of Ghana, griots bound one generation to the next.

The Quiet Disappearance of the Ghana Empire

Many may question how something so vast and powerful could vanish so easily. The capital of Koumbi Saleh hummed with life every night and day. However, the signs of decline were always there; they were just too subtle and quiet to be noticed easily. The merchant himself could notice how big disputes among local chiefs had grown ever since he first set foot in the city. There were also rumors saying tribute did not arrive to the king as fast as it had before. The merchant heard complaints from a certain northern trader who lamented the higher tolls imposed on the routes. Meanwhile, in the southern markets, whispers circulated of rising powers elsewhere where trade was said to be cheaper and gold easier to move.

Some believe the decline of the empire had to do with how the gold shifted. The mines in the east, beyond the reach of the Ghana Empire, had changed the trade routes. Without the arrival and departure of these merchants, the empire began to see a decrease in its flow of wealth. Others pointed their fingers at strange weather patterns that eventually brought the empire to its knees. Droughts visited the region longer and harsher than ever before. With its depleting wealth, the central government was unable to help all of those affected. The once-loyal territories were left with no choice but to fend for themselves.

Of course, there were also cracks from within the government itself. Ghana's strength had always relied on its balance between the king and his council and the capital and the provinces. However, during its later years, the empire found itself embroiled in succession disputes. In some regions, local leaders grew so bold that they unsheathed their weapons and clashed with their neighbors for control.

In the end, the Ghana Empire's foundations were shaken to their core. In the years to come, other kingdoms would rise. The 11th century saw the Almoravids, a Muslim Berber dynasty from North Africa, invade the region, which further weakened the empire. Then came the Sosso Kingdom and, afterward, the Mali Empire under Sundiata Keita. The Songhai Empire would also expand its territories, incorporating the Ghana Empire and shifting the maps once again. But still, Ghana's story lived on, forever immortalized in songs, rituals, and tales.

Chapter 2 – The Lost Legacy of the Mali Empire

Sundiata Keita had a rather rough beginning. He was born into a noble family within the Mandinka people of the Kangaba Kingdom. The Mandinka were a western Mandé-speaking nation. However, being one of the sons of Maghan Kon Fatta, the king of Kangaba, his path was full of obstacles. Although there existed a prophecy that talked about Sundiata's rise as a ruler, not everyone believed in him. After all, he was famously known for his inability to walk during his early childhood—a clear sign of weakness in the eyes of many. Some also claimed that he was able to walk as he aged but that he suffered from some sort of physical impairment, which eventually became one of the reasons why he was spared during conflicts. Meanwhile, his brothers were executed by opposing rulers.

Trouble brewed when West Africa saw the rise of a powerful Sosso king named Sumanguru Kanté. Apart from attacks launched on the Mandinka territories, including Kangaba, this new king also attempted to impose trade restrictions on the Mandinka. Sumanguru was well aware of the danger that Sundiata could bring to his rule. Not only did he have a legitimate royal bloodline, but he also had a prophecy surrounding him. So, the king captured Sundiata, as well as his mother and siblings. They were forced into political exile. Other accounts suggest that his mother, Sogolon, willingly took Sundiata and his siblings into exile, hoping they could escape the persecution or threats imposed by the tyrannical king.

Sundiata remained in exile for over two decades. During this period, he quietly built his strength and numbers, hoping he could one day return to his homeland and free his people. He successfully formed alliances with neighboring Mandinka peoples and eventually went against Sumanguru Kanté at the Battle of Kirina in 1235. Sundiata crushed the Sosso threat and accomplished his mission to unite the Mandé peoples under a single banner. It was here, on the blood-soaked plains, that the continent saw the first foundation of the Mali Empire being laid.

A drawing depicting Malian forces.'

Sundiata had finally realized the prophecy, as he became the first ruler of the Mali Empire. However, Sundiata knew he should not let conquest alone define his rule. He had experienced what it was like to live in a kingdom full of turmoil and political dangers, which gave him a clear understanding of what made kingdoms last. Sundiata built alliances with surrounding clans and rebuilt the destroyed city of Niani near the Sankarani River, which he later turned into his capital and a thriving trade hub that attracted both African and Arab traders alike.

There is a reason why Sundiata Keita's name is remembered as one of the wealthiest rulers of his time. Under his guidance, the goldfields of Bambouk and Wangara enriched Mali. Salt caravans streamed from the Sahara, and ivory, textiles, kola nuts, and copper all passed through the empire's markets, where tax collectors watched with keen eyes. In just less than a decade after the Battle of Kirina, Mali enjoyed relative peace, political unity, and economic growth. Mali's control of the trade routes undoubtedly contributed to the empire's growing wealth. By the 1240s, the Mali Empire was recognized as a major power in West Africa.

Apart from trade, Sundiata had his attention on human rights. The ruler famously created one of the first charters of human rights, known as the Manden Charter or Kouroukan Fouga. This oral charter was passed down by generations of Mandinka. It did not only speak about peace within diverse nations but also about the abolition of slavery, education, food security, and environmental protection.

As Mali expanded its borders, the empire found itself increasingly drawn into the orbit of Islam. Just like many other kingdoms and empires on the continent, the religion arrived not via fierce warriors or determined missionaries but with traders. Berber merchants from the north had long crossed the Sahara with salt, textiles, and finely copied Arabic books, exchanging them for West Africa's gold and goods. These merchants also brought their faith.

Islam did not replace the animist traditions of the locals. The Mandinka people remained deeply tied to their land, the spirits, and their ancestors. Even Sundiata Keita, though respectful of Islam, never failed to uphold the spiritual customs of his people. The king welcomed Muslim traders with open arms as long as they did not seek to disrupt the balance of the land. Of course, as Mali continued to grow over the years, the people witnessed the gradual growth of Islamic influence, especially among the elite. The ruling class spoke in Mandinka, but Arabic became the language of religion, legal systems, and higher learning.

By the time Mansa Uli (Sundiata's son) inherited the throne, Islam was no longer just a guest in the empire. The faith had become a part of its identity. Islamic education became an important part of both elite and urban life. It was common for young boys and men, especially those belonging to wealthy or scholarly families, to learn the Quran. Education in Mali often began with basic memorization of the Quran. More advanced students learned Arabic grammar, Islamic law (sharia), theology, mathematics, and astronomy. Education in rural areas varied. Compared to the major urban and trading centers, where Islamic education was highly valued, Islamic learning spread rather slowly and often coexisted with traditional animist practices in rural areas.

It is safe to say the legacy of the Mali Empire grew with each passing monarch (or mansa). However, Mansa Musa, who rose in the early 14th century, brought the Mali Empire to new heights. If Sundiata had laid the foundation, it was Mansa Musa who built the palaces upon it, widened the roads, raised the banners, and sent Mali's name across deserts and seas.

A popular depiction of Mansa Musa drawn on a medieval world map, the Catalan Atlas.'

Mansa Musa's court dazzled local chiefs and foreign emissaries. His reign was marked by material wealth, but this was not all. Mansa Musa, who was popularly known to be deeply devoted to Islam, made sure his empire became a strong bridge between sub-Saharan Africa and the wider Islamic world. He established formal diplomatic ties with the Mamluk Sultanate in Egypt and the rulers of Tunis and Morocco.

To put it simply, Mali's reputation among powerful Islamic states was greatly elevated under Mansa Musa. Mali's name entered Arabic chronicles as more than a footnote. These diplomatic relationships benefited the empire's economy and trade. Gold, salt, ivory, and enslaved laborers flowed through its cities. Scribes, poets, and scholars also traveled along the same routes, enriching the empire not just in wealth but also in wisdom.

The year 1324 was an important one for Mansa Musa. In Islam, there are five pillars that guide a believer's life. The first one was the declaration of faith (Shahada), daily prayer (Salat), giving charity (Zakat), fasting during the month of Ramadan (Sawm), and the pilgrimage to Mecca (Hajj). The last pillar only becomes compulsory if a person fulfils everything else. They have to be of sound mind and body, possess sufficient wealth to fund the journey, and ensure that their family and obligations at home would not suffer in their absence. Mansa Musa, who was considered one of the richest men of his time, met all these conditions with ease. With immense resources at his disposal and no obstacles standing in his way, it was time for him to fulfil this sacred duty and journey to the holy city of Mecca.

Chroniclers in Cairo and Alexandria later described the scale of the pilgrimage, which was undeniably staggering. The Mansa brought along sixty thousand attendants and hundreds of camels carrying over a dozen tons of gold. This was not for tribute but rather for generosity. The ruler of the Mali Empire was said to have given alms in every city he passed. He visited the bustling markets of Cairo, Medina, and Mecca, where he gave away a generous amount of gold. Many claimed that his generosity was so great that he devalued gold itself, inadvertently causing inflation in Cairo that lasted over a decade. When Mansa Musa learned of this, he reportedly apologized when he passed through Cairo again. Mansa Musa also funded the construction of mosques on his pilgrimage.

While some saw his actions as merely spending, others saw him strategically investing. Mansa Musa managed to forge more diplomatic ties. He met and hired scholars, brought back talented architects, and sowed admiration for the Mali Empire across the vast Islamic world.

Mansa Musa finished his pilgrimage sometime around 1235. However, instead of journeying straight home, he made a deliberate detour. He turned his caravan toward Gao, the rising capital of the Songhai people. Songhai was not yet the empire it would later become after the rise of powerful leaders like Sunni Ali and Askia Muhammad. Yet, Gao was already growing into a valuable trading post due to its location along the bend of the Niger River. After recognizing its strategic and economic significance, Mansa Musa worked to incorporate Gao into his domain. It is plausible that this was achieved through a blend of tribute, diplomacy, and some military pressure. Songhai retained a measure of local autonomy and acknowledged Mali's supremacy during Mansa Musa's reign. This political arrangement helped stabilize the eastern trade routes and fed goods and taxes into the Mali Empire's imperial treasury.

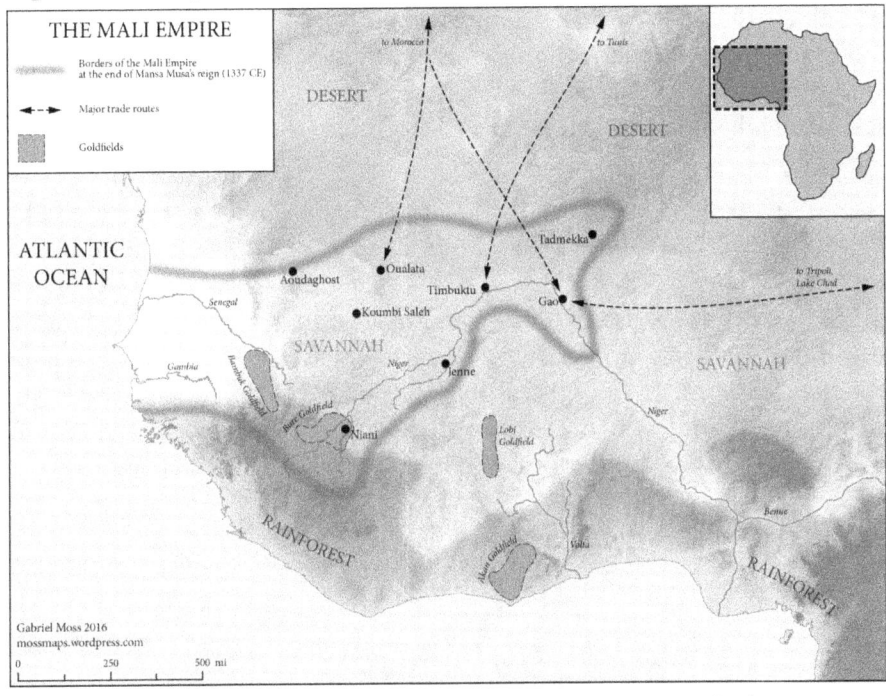

THE MALI EMPIRE

Borders of the Mali Empire at the end of Mansa Musa's reign (1337 CE)

Major trade routes

Goldfields

DESERT

to Morocco

to Tunis

DESERT

to Tripoli, Lake Chad

ATLANTIC OCEAN

Tadmekka

Oualata

Aoudaghost

Timbuktu

Gao

Koumbi Saleh

Senegal

SAVANNAH

Gambia

Niger

Jenne

SAVANNAH

Bure Goldfield

Niani

Lobi Goldfield

Niger

Benue

RAINFOREST

Volta

Ako Goldfield

RAINFOREST

Gabriel Moss 2016
mossmaps.wordpress.com

0   250   500 mi

The extent of the Mali Empire at the end of Mansa Musa's reign.⁵

This was not the end of Mansa Musa's travels. He also had his attention on Timbuktu. This city used to be a modest Saharan outpost known only to passing caravans, but it was further elevated by the Malian ruler, who saw its potential as both a thriving trade hub and a seat of learning. The merchants and scholars who traveled to Timbuktu might have imagined a humble city full of dusty huts. However, after Mansa Musa's contributions, they found an imperial city rising from the sands. Timbuktu was home to bustling markets, well-planned streets, and the majestic Djinguereber Mosque, which showcased the wonder of Sahelian architecture. Although the mosque was constructed mainly from mudbrick and timber, the structure stood with the grandeur of a stone cathedral. It was designed by an Andalusian architect named Abu Ishaq al-Saheli. Mansa Musa had met him during his pilgrimage. He recruited Abu Ishaq by paying him 40,000 mithqals of gold (equivalent to about 170 kilograms of gold).

The architecture of Mali was neither ostentatious nor basic. The many mosques that dotted the empire stood proudly like earthen monuments. They typically featured thick walls to resist desert heat, along with wooden beams that jutted into the sky. Mali's palaces were not adorned with marble or gold, despite the land being known for its endless deposits of natural minerals. However, they impressed visitors with their broad courtyards, shaded arcades, and completely unique designs. Mali's urban centers thrived not in spite of their geography but because of it.

Mansa Musa's ambition was not limited to conquest, wealth, bricks, and mortar. The ruler of the Mali Empire also knew the value of knowledge and wisdom. He never hesitated to spend his wealth on education. Mansa Musa played a hand in elevating the Sankoré Madrasa, a mosque that was turned into a center of Islamic scholarship. It later became known as the University of Sankoré. As time passed, the university became known as one of the most respected institutions of learning in the Islamic world, eventually rivalling Cairo and Fez in prestige.

Part of the Djinguereber Mosque today.'

A postcard with an image of the Sankoré Madrasa.[7]

For years, students across North Africa and even the Middle East traveled to the city to study in Timbuktu. Even Mali's own elites sent their sons to Timbuktu to study Quranic verses and master Islamic jurisprudence. Here, scholars taught and studied law, astronomy, mathematics, theology, and medicine. This was also where scribes would meticulously copy thousands of manuscripts in Arabic and local languages. These manuscripts ranged from treatises and poetry to histories and religious commentaries that were meant to be preserved across generations.

Like every other story of the past, Mali had a few pages of lesser-known episodes. There were whispers about a mysterious side of Timbuktu. Legend has it that the city was protected by a djinn. Known by the local population as Alfarouk, the mystical protector was said to have often appeared patrolling the city on his white horse. Alfarouk would be dressed in white clothes with a white turban wrapped neatly around his head.

He would only appear late at night. The djinn typically started his patrol at the cemetery of Saeriekeina. From here, he would ride his white steed across the city, visiting and inspecting every little corner and winding streets, from the University of Sankoré to the Djinguereber Mosque, where he would take a quick rest, to the markets of Timbuktu. Few could claim they had encountered the protector djinn, but those who did stumble upon him claimed that Alfarouk did nothing except order them to return to their houses.

There was another legend that revolved around Mali's gold. Perhaps influenced by the Mandé's ancient beliefs, gold was thought to be more than just a precious metal. The locals believed that it was spiritually protected and anyone who stole it or misused Mali's sacred wealth would be cursed to madness and misfortune. These stories might seem superstitious to the rational person. Perhaps it was nothing more than just echoes of animist traditions wrapped in Islamic garb. However, in the Mali Empire, the spiritual and material often walked side by side.

While both Sundiata Keita and Mansa Musa's names are remembered by many as two of the most influential leaders of West Africa, there are other often overlooked figures who left their marks—both positive and negative—on the Mali Empire.

Back when Mansa Musa set out on a journey to Mecca, he entrusted the empire to his son, Maghan I. However, Maghan was not the same as his father; he proved to be neither as wise nor as capable as Mansa Musa. After Mansa Musa's death around 1337, the throne was formally passed to Maghan I (who then adopted the name Mansa Maghan). However, there was no change in his leadership capabilities. Although he ruled only for four years, the Mali Empire saw a few glimpses of its decline. For instance, the empire's control over its distant territories began to loosen under Mansa Maghan's reign.

The new mansa was also criticized when he failed to prevent the escape of two important Songhai princes, Ali Kolon and Sulayman Nar. These two royals had been taken hostage during their father's campaigns years prior. With freedom finally in their hands once more, the two princes returned to Gao, where they eventually reestablished Songhai's independence and sowed the seeds of a future rival empire.

Considering the troubles that brewed during his reign, it is not a surprise that Mansa Maghan would be embroiled in a palace coup. According to traditional Mandé succession customs, the rightful heir to the throne was not necessarily the son of the king but rather the eldest male member of the ruling dynasty. In this case, that was Sulayman, the brother of Mansa Musa.

However, when Mansa Musa was preparing for his pilgrimage, he passed over his brother and instead appointed his own son, Maghan, as regent and eventual successor. But with Mali beginning to show signs of weakness under Maghan's rule, Sulayman decided to make his move. He succeeded in claiming the throne sometime in 1341. Although details of how exactly he did so remain murky, the historian Nehemia Levtzion suggests that Sulayman might have deposed his nephew to restore order and reclaim what was rightfully his. From here on, Maghan disappeared from the records, replaced by deeds done by Sulayman as the new ruler of the Mali Empire.

Sulayman strengthened Mali's diplomatic ties, particularly with North African states like the Marinid Sultanate of Morocco. He also succeeded in maintaining a firm grip over trade routes and internal administration. Unlike his nephew, Sulayman was known for his careful governance and measured leadership, keeping the empire's wealth and prestige intact. He also upheld the Islamic character of the court, continuing the legacy of his brother, Mansa Musa. This stability was not meant to be forever, though. Following his passing, the empire was thrown into the beginning of its fall.

Of course, the mansas were not the only main characters in the story of Mali. The empire was also held together by a network of intermediaries, such as guild leaders, ritual specialists, hereditary scribes, and merchant families who managed regional affairs and ensured the flow of goods, taxes, and loyalty. More often than not, these lesser-known figures were the ones who influenced the mansa's decisions.

Among them were the Sufi orders. These mystical Islamic brotherhoods began to spread across the region by the 12th century. They were devoted to spiritual devotion, education, and community leadership. These brotherhoods typically gained widespread popularity in cities like Timbuktu, Djenné, and beyond. Revered Sufi leaders, often called marabouts, acted as moral authorities, mediators, and advisors, sometimes even guiding rulers in matters of governance and diplomacy. Although there was never a case where they overthrew kings or ran the empire directly, their influence was very critical. Their endorsement could lend a ruler religious legitimacy, but their quiet withdrawal could erode loyalty among the people.

The Decline of Africa's Wealthiest Empire

Oral traditions and historical reconstructions repeatedly describe how Mansa Musa grew more cautious during his later years. The reason behind this was never confirmed, but scholars suggest that after his extravagant generosity during the Hajj, he had finally realized the burden of Mali's fame and the fragility that came with such immense wealth. External powers had become more aware of his empire's riches, opening the door to future hostilities from ambitious neighbors or envious factions within his own realm.

True, his empire endured and thrived following his death. However, the Mali Empire never reached the same heights when it was under Mansa Musa's reign. By the late 14th and early 15th centuries, the golden glow that had long dazzled the Mali Empire began to flicker. Historians point to the usual suspects, such as succession crises and overextended borders. Provinces once loyal to the empire began to grow restless. They eventually regained their independence and began carving away at the Mali Empire's eastern territories.

Following this, the empire also saw the rise of new trading powers. Shifting routes toward the Atlantic coast left Mali increasingly isolated. The goldfields were no longer full to the brim like they were centuries prior. With its resources dwindling and trade networks shifting, Mali found its economy greatly weakened over the years. Even the empire's famed cities like Timbuktu, Gao, and Djenné were no longer safe under the mansa's control. The Mali Empire's political structure was also on the brink of collapse by the 15th century. Local governors and vassal rulers, emboldened by the central government's weakness, began ruling their provinces as independent lords rather than loyal subjects. Things got worse when the continent saw the rise of the Songhai Empire, which did not waste a second to take advantage of the Mali Empire's fragility.

By the 16th century, the Mali Empire was no longer the envy of the world. It was reduced to nothing more than just a small kingdom clinging to fragments of its past glory. The empire that had once captivated the Islamic world with caravans of gold, mosques of knowledge, and kings of immeasurable wealth had fallen. Perhaps this was the very scene that Mansa Musa had once foreseen.

Chapter 3 – The Enigmatic Empire of Kanem-Bornu

The sun had just risen, slowly brightening the skies, and messengers had already arrived in the city of Birni Ngazargamu. They had traveled for days, enduring the unpredictable heat of the land. Their goal was to deliver scrolls, each sealed with symbols of distant governors, to Mai Idris Katakarmabe, a respected member of the Safawa dynasty, who ruled over Bornu in present-day northeastern Nigeria.

Once he received the scrolls, the mai (a term given to rulers of the Kanem-Bornu Empire) wasted no time in reading each of them. He stood at the edge of the courtyard, his face bearing a mix of expressions. These documents contained some good news, such as tributes that had been successfully collected, roads being cleared, and markets being reopened. There was also troubling news. A feud had reignited near the southern border. The reports suggested growing unrest among the western clans, which could potentially lead to a bigger conflict in the future.

There was silence in the air. It was clear that the court was nervous about what the future would hold.

"Worry not," Mai Idris might have said to reassure his officials. "We have come so far, and this is not the time to turn back."

This was not the first time his kingdom had faced storms; hardship was no stranger to the empire, especially since its earlier years in Kanem. His father had ruled during a period of chaos, and his grandfather had died trying to hold together a realm that was already falling apart. The state of the kingdom that Mai Idris inherited was slightly better than when his predecessors were on the throne. Yet, it was still fragile. Those in the court were right to feel nervous. Each of them remembered how the mighty Kanem kingdom had once been driven from its heartland.

Where It All Began

Long before the Saifawa reestablished their legacy in Birni Ngazargamu, they had a different homeland near the shores of Lake Chad. This inland sea was vast and temperamental, but its role as a life source in the Sahel drew settlers to its edges. In a land otherwise marked by arid plains and unpredictable rains, the lake offered more than just fish. There was fertile soil and grazing lands for animals all year-round. To its west, one could find open grasslands that stretched into savannahs, while the east gave way to dunes and desert. It was here, in this crossroads between ecosystems and trade routes, that one of Africa's earliest and most enduring kingdoms began to take shape—the Kingdom of Kanem.

The origins of the earliest political structures of Kanem are a topic of discussion, especially since they are preserved only in oral traditions and incomplete Islamic chronicles. Some scholars suggest that the kingdom's first rulers had connections to the Tubu, nomadic herders and warriors from the deserts of northern Chad and southern Libya. Others point to groups like the Zaghawa or possibly even an older but now-forgotten culture. Regardless, we could be certain that it was only by the 8th or 9th century that communities near Njimi (east of the lake) began to consolidate under a central authority. This early formation marked the foundation of Kanem—a kingdom that would one day be ruled and expanded by the Saifawa dynasty.

Much like the early rulers of Kanem, the Saifawa also had a rather hazy origin. Some traditions claim they descended from a noble Arab figure named Saif ibn Dhi Yazan, who had been sent from the Islamic heartlands to civilize the region. We can never be certain of this, but one thing we can be sure of is that the Saifawa were able to quickly establish themselves as the dominant ruling dynasty in Kanem by the 11th century.

With the Saifawa in control, the loose network of kinship-based communities in the region gradually transformed into a structured state. The dynasty established Njimi as its capital. On top of the hierarchy were none other than the Saifawa monarchs, who bore the title mai.

They were the ones who oversaw the kingdom's expansion across the Sahel. Under the mai were local leaders from various powerful clans.

Kanem's location also allowed the kingdom to rise as an important trade center. Caravans coming from Fezzan, Tripoli, and Egypt would typically pass through the kingdom carrying an array of goods and resources like salt, dates, horses, and fine cloth. These merchants often sought slaves, ivory, ostrich feathers, and local grains—all of which the lakeside communities could provide in abundance. Wealth flowed into the Kingdom of Kanem, and with it came new ideas, technologies, and the growing awareness of the wider Islamic world.

Yet even as Kanem thrived, its stability was never absolute. Tensions arose on the border. The Bulala, a fierce group of people from the east, conducted raids on the borders. By the mid-14th century, their numbers had multiplied and their strength had grown, transforming them into an unstoppable force. The Saifawa court at Njimi, after ruling Kanem for centuries, was eventually forced to abandon the capital. The dynasty fled westward across Lake Chad, where they rebuilt from the ground up at Bornu. They did not want to leave behind their ancestral lands and sacred shrines, but they saw no other way out.

Although the people of Kanem could experience some peace after their move to the western side of Lake Chad, Mai Idris knew it was not yet time to rest easy. He refused to sit still until Bornu could reclaim what Kanem had lost.

Rebuilding What Was Broken

To say that Njimi's fall in the mid-14th century splintered the kingdom is an understatement. The collapse of the Saifawa capital sent shockwaves across Kanem to the point where not only did it shatter the royal court, but it also triggered multiple episodes of power struggles across its provinces. Some clans were clever enough to take advantage of the situation. As the Saifawa fled, they wasted no time in claiming their independence. However, not all clans did this, as there were a few who chose to cling to the dynasty, hoping they could earn protection from any outside threats.

Indeed, the Saifawa had regained their influence after their escape, but Mai Idris knew that reunification would not come swiftly. After all, the clans in the western regions of Bornu had already grown accustomed to ruling themselves. Convincing them to submit once more to central rule required not only military credibility but also a willingness to acknowledge their customs and political weight.

So, the Saifawa court began strategizing. They decided to recognize key clan leaders as official governors. These titles were granted by the king himself, but they were carried out locally. This gave the appearance of royal authority while still allowing regional leaders to retain influence over their own people. There were also instances where the Saifawa resorted to intermarriage in order to cement loyalty. Islam also played an important role here. Although Islam had already taken root in the region centuries prior, the Saifawa's strong Islamic identity helped create a common ground. The use of Islamic law, the Arabic language, and the shared respect for scholars gave the court legitimacy that went beyond ethnicity or tribal lines.

Ruins of a fortress in Kanem-Bornu constructed during the reign of Mai Idris Alooma.'

Over time, the Saifawa saw their plans bear fruit. One chieftain after another eventually agreed to rejoin the state—some did so after reaching a compromise, while others fell to pressure. The kingdom's economy depended heavily on caravan taxation (especially salt and slave routes), control of oases and market towns, and seasonal pastoral movements. With tribes from the west and southwest pledging their allegiance to Bornu, the court could finally restore control over the economic and political networks that once held the kingdom together.

Work on the capital, Birni Ngazargamu, also took place. The Saifawa constructed new royal halls, launched coin-minting initiatives, and revived the imperial bureaucracy. Orders now flowed from a clear center. Up to this point, people began to speak of the kingdom as one again. Bornu became the true heir to Kanem's legacy.

By the end of the 1370s, everything was in place. The western clans were loyal, there was peace on the southern frontiers, and trade had recovered, bringing in even more wealth to the empire. For the first time in decades, the mai could finally taste unity, which was achieved not by fear but by structure.

However, not all of the wounds had healed completely. The Bulala still held firm to the east, across Lake Chad, and Mai Idris had not forgotten them. Skirmishes occasionally occurred along the eastern frontier. Plus, how could the people ever forget the ones who once drove them away from their homeland and crushed their once-thriving capital? Patrols were stationed near the lakeshore, with the envoys keeping a close watch on the enemy. But despite the rebirth of the empire, Bornu was not yet ready for a full-scale reconquest campaign. This mission would be reserved for the successors of Mai Idris. One day, when the time was right, the Saifawa would have their revenge.

Power on Horseback

As his empire continued to stabilize, Mai Idris Katakarmabe made it his utmost priority to improve the state of his military power. He understood that military power was not only a tool for defense but also a symbol of an empire's legitimacy. It could simply be proof that the Saifawa were no longer in retreat.

Bornu's strength, similar to Kanem before it, rested on the backs of horses. For centuries, the Saifawa took pride in their formidable cavalry. In contrast to the infantry of many neighboring kingdoms, Bornu's armies relied heavily on mounted troops, which were trained in both speed and discipline. The cavalry unit was tactically agile and fast-moving. Typically, the cavalry rode into battle in quilted armor or leather breastplates. At times, they were supported by iron-weapon-wielding elite guards. Together, these units formed the core of every major campaign.

An illustration of a Kanem-Bornu chief and his forces.[9]

Though detailed records from Idris's reign are limited, tradition and later practices suggest that he restructured and reinforced the cavalry. The royal court is believed to have established permanent cavalry units at key frontier zones. This way, they could respond faster to border tensions. It is plausible that the horses were bred locally and obtained through trade with northern merchants. The riders were drawn from both noble families and loyal clans who had pledged their loyalty to the Saifawa state.

Leibgardist des Scheiks von Bornu.

A depiction of a Kanem-Bornu cavalryman.[10]

It is safe to say the power of this military structure was not limited to its ability to suppress rebellions or defend the capital. It also allowed the empire to project power outward. With this military structure, the Kanem-Bornu Empire could secure trade routes, collect tribute in distant territories faster, and keep neighboring polities in check at all times. Raids against hostile groups were also common during these times, especially in areas where tax collection had lapsed or local rulers began testing the limits of central control.

Apart from the cavalry, some scholars also suggest that Mai Idris supported the development of fortified outposts and watchtowers. He might have also played a hand in improving internal roads that would benefit faster communication and troop deployment. Other military infrastructure, such as armories and stables, was built near Birni Ngazargamu and other strategic settlements. The court itself maintained a royal guard. It was made up of elite warriors who were tasked with protecting the king and his household.

Mai Idris Katakarmabe had successfully created more than just a defensive force by the end of his reign. He had restored the military spine of the empire, one strong enough to not only defend the empire but also intimidate its rivals. This undoubtedly laid the groundwork for bigger campaigns in the future, which were launched by his successors.

Mai Idris Alooma: The Empire's Most Celebrated Ruler

Mai Idris Alooma ascended the throne in 1570. He inherited an empire that was structurally sound, economically active, and militarily stable. Yet, the empire still had a long way to go before it could be the same as before. Alooma was a confident ruler, though; he was determined to not only reclaim lost prestige but also to transform Bornu into a power that could rival any in the region.

If one could summarize his military campaigns in only two words, they would be swift and strategic. One of his most important moves was to push eastward, going against the empire's main enemy, the Bulala. He never forgot how the Bulala drove his ancestors from Njimi two centuries earlier; it was high time for Bornu to finally show its teeth and reclaim the ancestral lands of Kanem.

The campaign began with careful preparation. To do this correctly, he had to reorganize his forces. Alooma integrated new infantry tactics and reinforced his already formidable cavalry. Records also claimed that he adopted Ottoman-style firearms into his forces—a rare innovation in the region at the time. It was said that he acquired the firearms through trade and diplomatic relations with the Ottoman Empire and North African powers. These firearms were limited in number, but they were crucial in his campaign as they provided a psychological edge in battle. Alooma even recruited Turkish and Arab gunmen to train his troops and established permanent military camps, sometimes with small cannons and matchlock guns. By doing this, he was able to reinforce his image as a modernizing ruler.

Of course, the war against the Bulala was not a single climactic battle. Instead, it involved a series of aggressive campaigns to the east of Lake Chad. Once Alooma and his forces made it into the former Kanem territory, they wasted no time in engaging the Bulala in open-field clashes and strategic raids. Alooma was able to gradually erode Bulala resistance through a combination of constant military pressure and the seizure of trade and supply routes.

Although Bornu remained his main seat of power, the success of reclaiming the old capital of Kanem was deeply symbolic. To many, it was viewed as a restoration of ancestral pride and a reminder that the Saifawa dynasty had been fully rejuvenated. However, Alooma's ambitions did not stop there. The mai also focused westward and northward, particularly the groups that had been threatening Bornu's long-distance trade.

One of his targets was the Tuareg. These nomadic raiders could typically be seen harassing and attacking caravans in the central Sahara on their fast-moving camels. If Alooma were to let this continue, it would disrupt the flow of salt, cloth, and horses from North Africa. Even worse, it could endanger diplomatic missions. Before these nuisances turned into a bigger conflict, Alooma made it a priority to deploy his elite cavalry squadrons to drive the Tuareg away from his realm. And so, the routes were secured once more.

Meanwhile, Alooma launched campaigns in the west, particularly into the Hausa city-states. He had his eyes fixed especially on the regions close to Kano and Katsina, which were growing in influence and wealth. Although these campaigns were not full conquests, they were launched to weaken resistance and assert Bornu's dominance. Alooma also did this to ensure that trade routes through Hausa territory remained accessible and taxed under Bornu's terms.

Farther south, Alooma's forces reinforced the borders against smaller kingdoms and nomadic groups that had begun pushing into Saifawa-controlled territory during earlier periods of instability. These border campaigns were less glamorous but still important. They had to be done in order to consolidate the empire's frontiers and protect the agricultural base that sustained its army and administration.

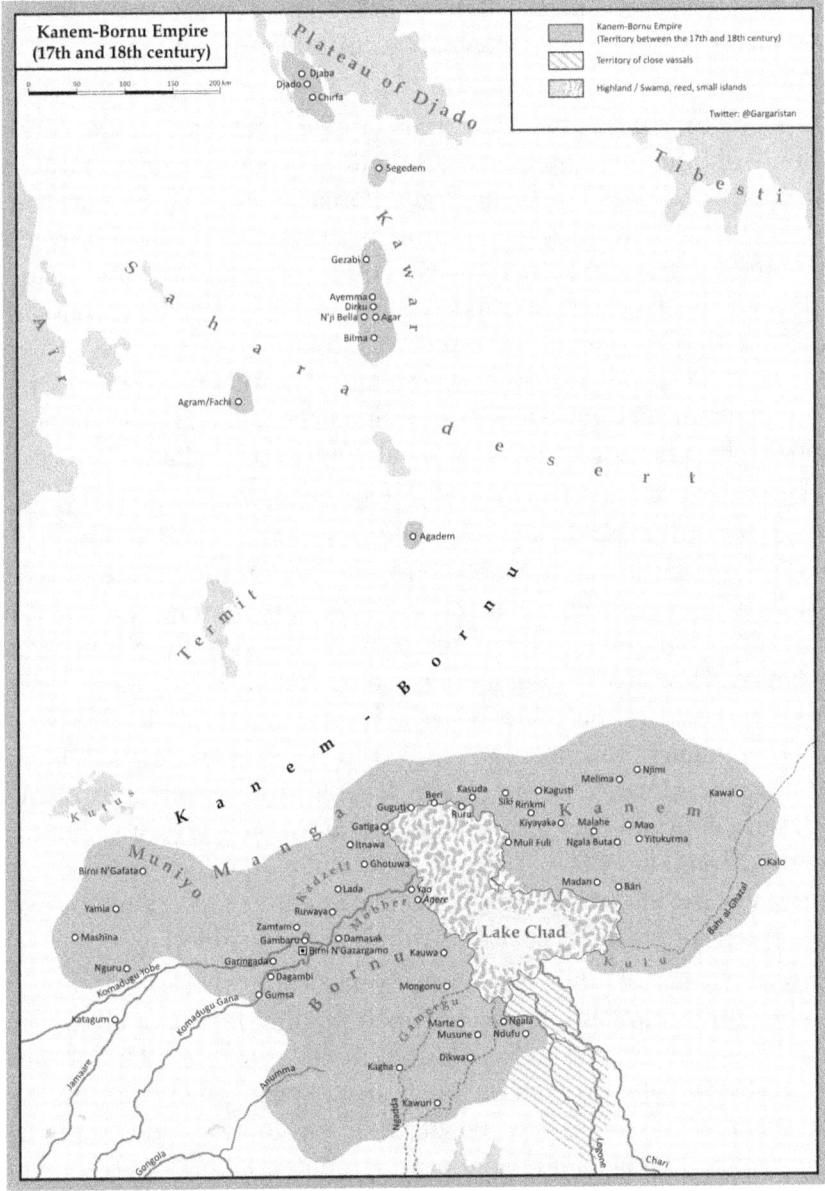

Map detailing the territories of Kanem-Bornu during the 17th century.[11]

Mai Idris Alooma was a powerful ruler, but he was not just a warrior king. Scholars agree that he was also a reformer who was deeply committed to Islamic principles and administrative efficiency. During his reign, the empire began to see the application of Sharia law more consistently. The mai also played a role in establishing Islamic courts that were responsible for handling legal matters based on Quranic guidance. Islamic judges (known as qadis) were appointed in reconquered areas to help integrate them under a unified religious and legal framework.

It is safe to assume that the administration flourished under Alooma. Not only did the mai implement a system of record-keeping, but he also succeeded in strengthening the court bureaucracy. The empire saw an increase in the construction of fortified roads and resthouses reserved for both soldiers and merchants. As a devoted Muslim, Alooma performed the Hajj; the specific year when he went on this pilgrimage remains a debate. Upon his return, the mai brought along respected scholars, books, and renewed diplomatic ties with him. These moves undoubtedly further enriched Bornu's intellectual life and positioned the empire to be a beacon of Islamic governance in sub-Saharan Africa.

However, it is also worth noting that the foundations of Alooma's Islamic reforms already existed centuries before. These foundations were laid by Mai Dunama Dabbalemi, who sat on the throne of Kanem from 1210 to 1224. The mai was credited with starting the kingdom's large-scale adoption of Islam. He corresponded with North African Muslim leaders, invited scholars and jurists to his court, and even sent emissaries on pilgrimages to Mecca. It was under his leadership that Islamic influence was able to spread rapidly through the elite and administrative classes. Almost similar to Mai Idris Alooma, his reign was also marked by military expansion east and south. He was known to have used Islam as both a spiritual guide and a diplomatic tool. By using this strategy, he succeeded in presenting Kanem as a legitimate Muslim polity, especially in the eyes of the wider Islamic world.

However, Islam did not erase what came before. Before the introduction of the faith, the Kanuri people (the dominant ethnic group in the region) followed indigenous spiritual traditions. They honored their ancestors, often sought guidance from spirit healers, and practiced rituals tied to nature. These beliefs did not entirely fade when Islam came; rather, they blended together with the new faith. This resulted in a distinctive synthesis. For instance, marabouts or Islamic spiritual leaders served as preachers, healers, and protectors. Quranic verses were also used in divination and healing practices, often alongside traditional herbs and charms. Moreover, many communities blended mosque-based practices with local traditions; this continued even during the reigns of deeply devoted Islamic rulers like Alooma.

This cultural merging extended into the arts. Kanuri folktales included Islamic influences. The same could be said of poetry, which told the feats of both kings and saints. This cultural synthesis led to the birth of a unique local literary tradition. Known as the Ajami script, this form of writing used the Arabic script to record African languages. Interestingly, people throughout Africa still use it to this day to write phonetic renderings of about a dozen languages, including Swahili and Wolof. As for Kanuri scholars in the empire, they used this to produce legal documents, historical accounts, and religious texts that preserved the intellectual heritage of the empire. Nevertheless, despite Arabic dominating both religious and diplomatic affairs, Kanuri remained the language of the people. It was the language spoken in markets, homes, and even court gatherings.

The Decline of the Kanem-Bornu Empire

It is rare for empires to fall overnight. More often than not, they erode slowly, either through war, change, time, or a combination of everything. Nothing is meant to last forever, and unfortunately, the same could be said of the Kanem-Bornu Empire. Up until the 17th century, the empire managed to endure centuries of conflicts and turmoil. It had reformed itself, eventually regaining its prestige under leaders like Mai Idris Katakarmabe and Mai Idris Alooma. However, even its resilience had limits.

Ironically, the earliest signs of decline did not come from the empire's enemies but from Mother Nature. Lake Chad was once the empire's lifeline, but over time, climate change and environmental stress changed this. As water levels dropped and farmland shrank, food shortages and local tensions increased. This new vulnerability was noticed by the empire's neighbors. Soon, nomadic incursions into Bornu's borders contributed to its decline. Meanwhile, the trans-Saharan trade, which had long been the empire's economic backbone, also began to shift toward European-controlled coastal trade routes. As the caravans slowed, Bornu began to lose revenue. With its wealth dwindling, its influence began to wane. As the years passed, the empire saw a major decrease in the number of scholars and foreign envoys in its court.

The empire also struggled internally during its later years. The once powerful Saifawa dynasty had grown weaker over time. Succession disputes often occurred. Coupled with the rising independence among regional governors, the empire could clearly see its foundation being shaken. Even the military, once a source of Bornu's pride, struggled to contain growing threats like the ones posed by the Fulani jihads in the 18th and 19th centuries, who swept across West Africa. Bornu resisted longer than most, but the pressure was relentless.

Some historians also pointed their fingers at Bornu's overreliance on hereditary rule and a stagnant bureaucracy. Others, on the other hand, blamed the weakening of scholarly institutions and the growing friction between syncretic traditions and reformist Islamic movements. The empire was once proud of its cultural flexibility, yet it became a source of tension.

It is sufficient to say that there was no single fall. It was just a gradual fading. The final blow came in 1893 when a Sudanese warlord named Rabah Zubairu sacked Birni Ngazargamu. This effectively ended the centuries of Saifawa rule.

Chapter 4 – The Mysteries of the Songhai Empire

The Mali Empire was still standing in the 15th century. In major cities like Niani, life continued as usual. The imperial court had no time to rest. Orders were dispatched day and night, coins were minted, and scholars were sent on pilgrimages or across the map to seek new knowledge that could potentially benefit the empire. Tribute caravans still passed through the desert routes, but security had grown weaker. At first, the caravans were only harassed, but over time, these attacks grew in both frequency and brutality.

These attacks and raids came from the Songhai. Following the escape of two Songhai princes—Ali Kolon and Sulayman Nar—to Gao many years prior, the Songhai had been growing in influence. Ali Kolon, who eventually became the ruler of his people, managed to reestablish Songhai independence, thus opening a way for them to slowly challenge the authority of the Mali Empire. These attacks began on a small scale. The Songhai typically struck in the night, targeting garrisons on the border and merchant trains. They also stole livestock and executed minor officials. However, as they grew bolder, so did their raids. By the 1440s, entire towns were being harassed. The attackers were usually organized, skilled, and relentless, like an army.

The Mali Empire could no longer ignore them. These attacks were taking a toll on the imperial court and had to be dealt with immediately.

The Origins of Songhai

The Songhai, also spelled as the Songhay, were part of a larger ethnolinguistic group that spoke Nilo-Saharan languages. They were distinct from their Mandé-speaking Mali neighbors to the west. Over centuries, they settled in what is now eastern Mali and western Niger, building towns and trading hubs that linked West Africa to the Saharan trade routes. Their ancestral home was Gao, which was transformed into a commercial center as early as the 9th century. With its location on a broad bend in the Niger River, where the desert met the floodplains, Gao was considered the midpoint between merchants from North Africa, the Sahel, and forest kingdoms to the south.

Of course, its reputation as a thriving commercial center soon attracted the attention of outsiders, particularly the leader of the Mali Empire, Sundiata Keita. Gao's independence was cut short when Sundiata embarked on an expansion campaign in the 13th century. With the Songhai region drawn into Mali's growing imperial orbit, Gao was seized and brought under Mali control. From then on, the Songhai kings were expected to pay tribute to the mansa. Despite being allowed to retain a level of autonomy, the Songhai kings were put under close watch. Mali stationed its own set of officials in Gao.

On the outside, Songhai might have seemed pacified. However, resistance was brewing underneath the surface. Not once did the people of Gao forget their own kings and the feeling of freedom to live on their lands without interference from outsiders. The Songhai always had their eyes open, waiting for even the smallest crack to appear on Mali's borders. That time came in the late 14th century when the empire had to deal with problems closer to home. Mali had to deal with succession crises, economic strain, and rebellions in core regions and western provinces like Takrur and parts of the Senegal River Valley. The empire had to divert its attention away from the eastern frontiers. It was the opportunity that the Songhai had been waiting for.

From Raids to an Empire: The Reign of Sunni Ali

Sunni Ali (sometimes known as Ali the Great) rose to power in 1464. Before he wore the crown, the Songhai's confrontation with Mali and its neighbors largely followed the pattern of seasonal raids. Their attacks were swift and strategic. Their purpose was mainly to disrupt and weaken instead of occupy. However, when the Mali Empire showed signs of weakness, Sunni Ali was quick to seize the chance. Instead of merely hitting and retreating, Sunni Ali told his forces to stand firm.

"The time when we test the waters has now passed," he might have said to his people. "Our enemy has weakened. Now is the time to move forward!"

And so, his campaigns began. The Songhai succeeded in consolidating towns and eastern trade routes, especially those along the Niger River. Their influence spread so much that the areas that had once paid tribute to Mali began shifting their allegiance. The Songhai targeted Timbuktu in 1468. At the time, Timbuktu was under the authority of the Tuareg. The Mali Empire had long lost its grip on the city of knowledge due to its own struggles, allowing the Berber nomadic people from the Sahara to take control of it. But when Sunni Ali and his forces arrived, the Tuareg failed to hold their ground. Timbuktu fell; this was considered the Songhai's first major prize.

A few years later (possibly in 1475), Sunni Ali gazed toward Djenné. Unlike Timbuktu, Djenné was still under the nominal control of the Mali Empire. For years, the city had been an important trade and intellectual center. However, with Mali's decline, its defense was on the brink of collapse. Taking advantage of this, Sunni Ali laid siege to the city. It lasted several months, but the Songhai ruler had a professional army by his side. While his armored cavalry was highly effective, especially with their speed, Sunni Ali also had a powerful naval fleet. This was also the very navy that he used to patrol the Niger River. The Songhai eventually won.

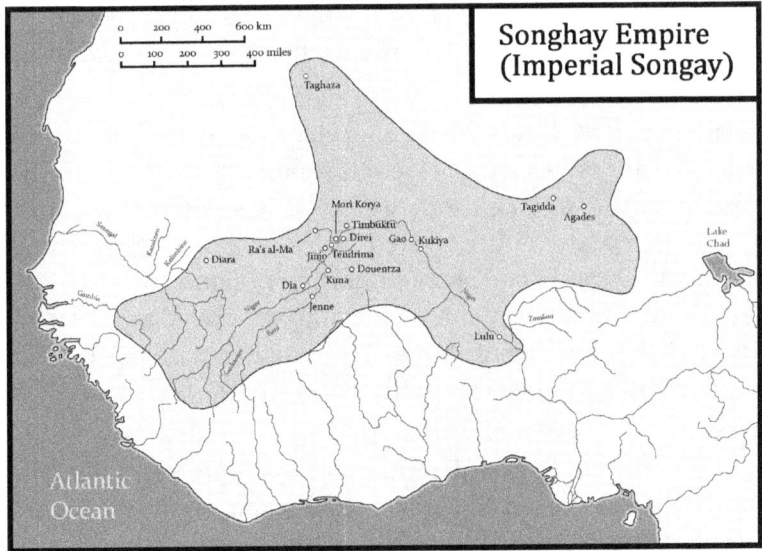

Map detailing the territories of the Songhai Empire.[13]

With more territories now in his hands, Sunni Ali knew it was time to focus on administration. He divided these newly acquired territories into provinces and appointed governors for each of them. These governors were known as fari, and they functioned as judges, tax collectors, and military commanders. While local chiefs were not expected to hand over their crowns, they had to pay tribute to the Songhai king. Of course, there were instances when hostages were taken from important families to ensure their loyalty and prevent any rebellions. Political marriages were also common.

Although there were cases when Sunni Ali offered rewards to those who chose to yield—many captured warriors were said to have been given places in his own ranks—his reputation as a ruthless leader endured for generations. His brutality could be seen in a certain episode where the Songhai came into conflict with members of the Fulbe tribe (a semi-nomadic group that settled in parts of the Middle Niger region). According to sources like the *Tarikh al-Sudan*, the leaders of the Fulbe attempted negotiations at first. However, Sunni Ali was unable to erase his deep suspicion toward them, especially since the Fulbe had strong ties to Islamic scholars.

Although the Songhai Empire officially adopted Islam, scholars claimed that Sunni Ali's personal beliefs were rather murky. Yes, he patronized Muslim scholars and even conducted state affairs with Islamic titles. However, at the same time, he never abandoned the animist traditions of the Songhai people. Oral accounts say he often invoked spirits, consulted seers, and led rituals that were far removed from Quranic orthodoxy.

This did not sit well with the Islamic elites. Scholars from Timbuktu's University of Sankoré especially viewed Sunni Ali as hostile to the faith. This was largely due to an episode where he was said to have persecuted clerics and purposely disrespected Islamic law. There were also accusations of the Songhai leader disguising political purges as religious judgment. The 17th-century chronicler and scholar from Timbuktu, al-Sa'di, despite acknowledging Sunni Ali's military brilliance, called the ruler a tyrant and an unbeliever in his work, *Tarikh al-Sudan*.

But back to the story of Sunni Ali and the Fulbe. To avoid future conflicts, the Songhai king ordered a violent suppression. The numbers were never confirmed, but historians suggest that some members of the Fulbe were executed, while those who survived were either dispersed or forcibly incorporated into the Songhai military's ranks. Because of this incident, Sunni Ali earned the nickname "Sunni the Merciless."

Sunni Ali was also known for ruling through fear as much as policy. Understanding the power of one's image, he made sure his enemies saw him not just as a king or a warrior. Sunni Ali wore the mask of a magician; he was said to have spread rumors about his own magical abilities. He claimed to have possessed multiple charms that could turn him invincible in battle or grant him the ability to call storms. Some even spoke of a leather talisman that the king wore under his armor that protected him from blades.

However, Sunni Ali did not always leave chaos in his wake. The king was also credited with investing in dykes and irrigation systems that greatly improved his empire's agriculture and food security. Trade in the region also recovered under his watchful eye. Taxes flowed, and roads were no longer full of nests of bandits. What had once been a loosely held territory along the river was quickly becoming a unified and centralized empire.

Sunni Ali sat on the throne for nearly three decades. He eventually passed in 1492 (possibly on November 6th), though his cause of death remains a debate among scholars and historians. Some oral traditions suggest the Songhai leader drowned in the Niger River as he was returning from a military campaign. There were also those who claimed that he was assassinated either by his own commanders or perhaps by factions within the royal court. If the second theory were true, Sunni Ali's own nephew, Muhammad Ture, would likely have been behind it.

Following Sunni Ali's death, the crown was passed to his son, Sunni Baru. However, Sunni Baru was almost similar to his father when it came to faith. He was seen by many in the Muslim scholarly class as an insufficiently devout Muslim. He was alienated by the religious elite of both Timbuktu and Gao. They preferred the throne to be given to Muhammad Ture, who appeared to be more of a devout Muslim. Knowing that he had support from Islamic clerics and influential merchant classes, Muhammad Ture challenged Sunni Baru's rule. This culminated in a decisive battle near Gao, where Sunni Baru was overthrown. This provided a clear path for Muhammad Ture to ascend to the throne. Adopting the name Askia Muhammad I, he founded the Askia dynasty. As for Sunni Baru, his name disappeared from historical sources shortly after his defeat. Scholars suggest he was either exiled or killed, which were common outcomes for deposed rulers at the time.

With Askia Muhammad on top of the hierarchy, it is not a surprise that Islam became increasingly more important in governance. Legal disputes, especially those related to trade, marriage, and inheritance, were settled using Sharia law, and taxation systems were set based on Islamic models of zakat (alms). It was also during the reign of Askia Muhammad that Timbuktu reached new heights. The city was already a renowned center of learning, trade, and Islamic devotion even before it was seized by Sunni Ali. Yet, under his reign, tensions often rose among the scholarly community. It was common for scholars to become imprisoned. Some fled the city itself, while others kept their heads down, constantly walking on eggshells so as not to provoke Sunni Ali's wrath.

However, when Askia Muhammad seized the throne, the scholars at Timbuktu were finally able to breathe easy. The empire not only restored the city's prestige but also expanded its intellectual reach. The University of Sankoré, which was one of the three main madrasas in Timbuktu, saw a rise in the number of scholars from across Africa and the Middle East. They could debate theology, law, astronomy, medicine, and mathematics without the fear of being silenced or punished once more. Timbuktu continued to become a city of manuscripts, as it housed an array of texts discussing different subjects from pharmacology to Islamic jurisprudence.

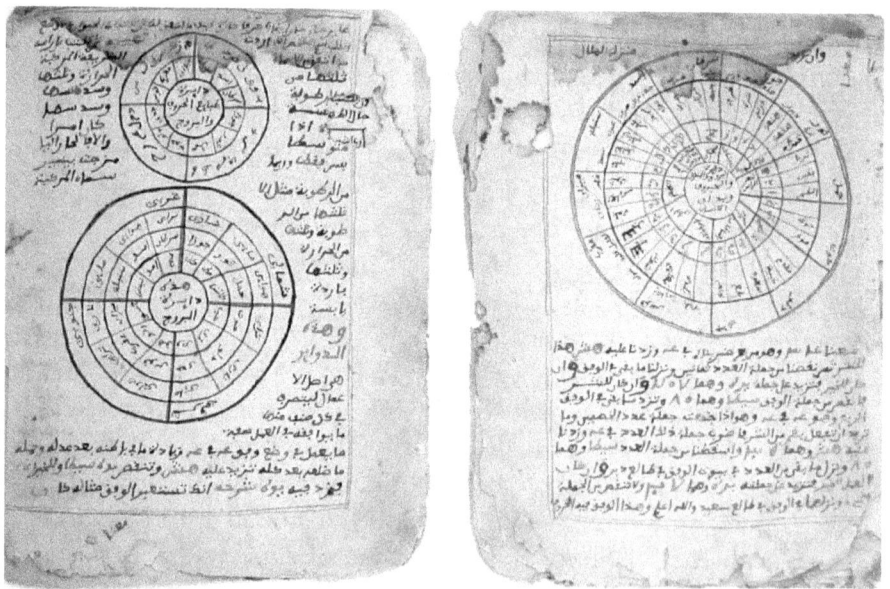

Timbuktu manuscripts written in Arabic about mathematics and astronomy.[18]

However, for all the intellectual flourishing in Timbuktu, one would expect that such a sophisticated empire would leave behind a detailed record of its own legacy. After all, its scholars copied legal documents, studied astronomy, and debated Islamic philosophy. Its cities produced treatises, correspondence, and tax registers. Yet, interestingly and mysteriously, no complete Songhai royal chronicle survives today.

The tomb of Askia in Gao.[14]

What survives today are only fragmentary accounts. These were not written by the Songhai court itself. Most of the time, they were by outsiders like Moroccan chroniclers, Arab merchants, and later European explorers. Much of what we know about the empire comes from works like the *Tarikh al-Sudan* and the *Tarikh al-Fattash*, both of which were actually written in Timbuktu after the Moroccan conquest. While these writings give us insights into the empire, they were filtered through the lens of foreign rule and post-collapse hindsight.

This disappearance of firsthand records raised countless questions. Did the Songhai kings never commission royal histories? Some scholars argued that they did. Those chronicles were presumably once kept in major cities in Gao and Djenné. Unfortunately, they were lost during the Moroccan invasion of 1591. Perhaps the Moroccans, in an effort to legitimize their rule and sever Songhai's link to its past, deliberately erased these records. Some also speculate that this erasure was done by internal factions after Sunni Ali's death. They might have done so to rewrite or obscure the deeds of their predecessors.

Others argue that despite their scholarly reputation, Songhai rulers might have preferred their stories to be preserved in oral tradition. In a realm where griots or oral historians were revered as walking libraries, it is very much possible that much of the empire's memory was never meant to be preserved in ink at all.

It is important to note that this case is not solved; these are nothing more than just speculations and theories. But whatever the cause, the loss is indeed profound. Without a clear timeline of reigns and without the voices of Songhai rulers or their scribes, historians are left with no choice but to reconstruct the empire's story only from fragments and echoes. The absence of a firsthand narrative voice has also created space for legends. Oral traditions often fill the gap with stories of magical kings, vanishing armies, and cursed tombs. Although these tales are rich in texture, they somehow also show how much of Songhai's history is incomplete.

What is almost complete is the story of how the Songhai Empire declined.

The Decline of the Songhai Empire

The year was 1591, and the Songhai Empire found itself on the brink of chaos. From what was once the undisputed power of West Africa, fully equipped with a formidable army and prosperous lands that stretched from the Atlantic coast to the fringes of the Sahara, the Songhai could practically see its decline in the near future. Here, on the plains near Tondibi (north of the Niger River), the empire was left with no other choice but to face its enemy.

Led by Sultan Ahmad al-Mansur of Morocco, the enemy pierced the borders from the north. The Moroccan troops were unlike any other force the Songhai had ever encountered before. The enemy had high morale, largely due to their recent victories against the Portuguese. The sultan dispatched a rather small force into the empire despite knowing the Songhai had tens of thousands of soldiers available.

However, this small force was lethal. At the forefront of the force was the Andalusian convert Judar Pasha, who was a Spaniard at birth but Muslim at heart. His troops carried matchlock rifles and light artillery. Each of them was also well-versed in European-style battlefield coordination. It is safe to say that the Moroccan troops represented a military revolution—gunpowder warfare—that was sweeping across Europe and parts of the Islamic world.

The Songhai, on the other hand, chose to remain loyal to the strategies of an earlier age. Yes, the empire's military numbers were immense, but the Songhai relied heavily on cavalry, swords, and traditional tactics. They were not familiar with gunpowder combat. The reasons behind this loyalty to age-old military traditions were complex. While some historians suggest a misplaced confidence in the strength of numbers, others argue that the Songhai was geographically isolated from gunpowder trade networks.

Although Songhai had vast territories, its interior location in West Africa meant it was isolated from the primary maritime trade routes that brought gunpowder weapons to North Africa, Europe, and the Middle East. While the Moroccan forces had direct access to firearms via their Mediterranean ports and alliances with the Ottomans and the Europeans, the Songhai had no consistent contact with such powers. Furthermore, overland trade routes across the Sahara were slow and risky, making them less suitable for transporting delicate technologies like firearms in bulk.

The two forces eventually clashed at Tondibi on March 13th, 1591. Instead of beginning with the sounds of swords clashing and gunpowder smoke taking over the air, the battle was opened with the Songhai driving a herd of armored cattle toward the Moroccan lines. This tactic was not new; they had been using cattle on the battlefield to disorient the enemy and break their formation.

This tactic worked well before, but not this time. The Moroccans perhaps had already studied their enemy tactics beforehand, as they remained calm. They released their shot in volleys. The crack of rifles and the smell of gunpowder soon fill the air, sending the cattle into a frenzy. Instead of trampling forward, however, these creatures retreated back to where they came from—the panicked cattle trampled straight into the Songhai ranks.

Then came the roars of the Moroccan cannons. The Songhai soldier had never faced such firepower. Their formations were disintegrated, and the soldiers' morale plummeted. Thousands chose to flee, knowing that it would be impossible to engage with the enemy in close combat. In just the blink of an eye, the great imperial army that had once swept across West Africa collapsed.

The Moroccans' victory at Tondibi cleared the path for them to advance. Many cities fell into their grasp without major resistance. This included Timbuktu, Djenné, and even the jewel of the Songhai Empire itself, Gao. In the aftermath of this invasion, Askia Ishaq II, the ruling emperor of Songhai at the time, was deposed. The court was then dissolved. Local resistance occurred throughout the region, but no unified response ever came.

Still, despite their huge victory, the Moroccan occupation would not last. After all, they had conquered a land that they did not understand. The trans-Saharan supply lines were stretched thin, and the Moroccans had troubles brewing in their homeland, especially as the Saadi dynasty declined. Then came episodes of mutiny; the Moroccan soldiers refused to carry out their orders due to poor pay and harsh conditions. At this point, it was clear that despite securing the major cities of Songhai, governing such a vast and decentralized territory from faraway Marrakesh proved logistically impossible.

The Moroccans eventually withdrew from the region by the late 1600s. Although some Moroccan-descended military elites remained in the region and eventually blended into local society, Moroccan influence had all but collapsed. Despite the withdrawal of the invaders, the Songhai never rose again.

Songhai's failure to benefit from the power vacuum left by the Moroccans stemmed not only from the blow at Tondibi but also from deeper fractures already present before the battle. The empire was fraught with succession disputes. Its over-centralized authority also contributed to its decline, as did the Songhai's reliance on traditional military doctrine. As time went on, the region saw the rise of many bold local rulers, former allies, and client states that dared to defy the central government and eventually declare their independence. The state was fragmented once again; the only difference this time was that no new ruler emerged who was strong enough to reunite the empire.

And so, the Songhai Empire was no more. The political vacuum was eventually filled by new powers like the Sokoto Caliphate.

Chapter 5 – Great Zimbabwe and the Lost Cities of Southern Africa

"How much farther?" one of the envoys asked as he swept the sweat off his forehead.

They had been traveling for many weeks. They had journeyed from the lowlands of the Limpopo, braved through the forests where leopards watched them in silence, and crossed the savannah where menacing vultures circled high overhead. They would surrender to their tiredness if they could, but they had a mission. These envoys hailed from a modest chiefdom in the Luangwa Valley far to the north. They were to deliver tribute, secure favor, and return to their homeland with stories of the fabled Great Zimbabwe.

"I think we are already here," another one of the envoys responded as he squinted his eyes.

There it was, the capital city of the Zimbabwe kingdom. Its stone walls loomed in the distance, appearing pale against the afternoon sun. The envoys, both relieved and impressed by the sight of such a grand city, wasted no time in continuing their journey. They traversed along the hill path, moving in the direction of the gates of Great Zimbabwe. As they got closer, the envoys began to see life. They passed herders leading cattle across terraced hillsides. They could hear the laughter of children who were playing and kicking gourds beneath the baobab trees. The outer walls were undoubtedly impressive. Not only were they hugging the terrain in graceful curves, but they were also constructed without mortar.

It was as if they had grown from the earth.

When the envoys finally entered the gates, the tales they heard of the city seemed suddenly less exaggerated. They were greeted by order. It was not a city of only reed huts. The courtyards were swept clean, and couriers could be seen moving quickly between dwellings, some of which were built of mud and others of stone.

Of course, the envoys could not miss the main highlight of the city itself. Towering above them all was none other than the Hill Complex, which was likely its religious core. Possibly the oldest part of the city, the Hill Complex was perched atop a rocky outcrop, overlooking the surrounding valley. Some said it was once accessible only through narrow passageways. Given its position and seclusion—it featured narrow, maze-like corridors and symbolic stonework—scholars believe it might have been the very location where ceremonial or royal functions were held. Perhaps this was where sacred rites were performed or where the king sought counsel from rainmakers and spiritual advisors.

A view of the Hill Complex from the valley.[15]

There was also the Great Enclosure, which many consider to be the most iconic and impressive structure of Great Zimbabwe. This stone elliptical wall was so massive that it seemed to defy both time and space. Its remnants can still be seen today. Encircled by a high outer wall of carefully laid granite blocks—some reaching over ten meters in height—this elliptical space likely served as the residence of the ruling elite. Other than platforms and turrets, the Great Enclosure also had a conical tower, though its exact function remains unknown. While some speculate that it was built to impress, many others believed the tower once held symbolic meaning, possibly related to fertility, authority, or even cosmology.

The envoys arrived at the Valley Ruins, which spread outward from these royal and elite centers. This was where the majority of the people lived. Here, they saw women weaving cloth or creating shell jewelry. Other people tended to goats in neatly fenced yards. The houses were usually built using *daga* (mud) and thatch, and their homes were arranged in clusters that reflected family or clan units. Modern archaeologists uncovered hearths, tools, and livestock pens, which point to a vibrant urban life. The commoners in Great Zimbabwe typically worked on their fields. Others were professionals in ironworking.

Aerial view of the Great Enclosure and Valley Complex.[16]

What remains of the conical tower within the Great Enclosure.[17]

The envoys also made their way to the markets, where traders from across the continent were said to meet. From Swahili merchants and their beautiful coral beads to the Arabs with their caravans full of textiles to local artisans who worked on their shiny wares, the markets were alive with activity. For nearly an hour, the envoys marveled at how structured everything was. How could a kingdom so grand exist in a place where maps showed nothing, one of them may have thought to himself.

Behind every kingdom stood the king. He wielded not only political authority but also spiritual reverence. The same could be said of Great Zimbabwe. Despite the lack of written records that survived—if there were any to begin with—we can never be sure of the name of these rulers. Nevertheless, oral traditions and archaeological findings suggest the city was ruled by a monarch who was seen as semi-divine.

Rainmakers were also important figures. Believed to possess the power to intercede between the heavens and the earth, the rainmakers could call forth rain through rituals and ancestral invocation. In a kingdom that relied on agriculture, it is not a surprise that a rainmaker's role was considered important. The people depended on them to bring rainfall, which could nourish their crops and fields. Archaeological evidence, such as clay figurines and ritual objects found near the Hill Complex, suggests that ceremonies linked to rain and fertility were conducted near or within elite compounds, possibly under royal supervision. Today, Great Zimbabwe is remembered by local communities surrounding the region as not only a royal city but also as a revered rainmaking shrine.

Some have proposed the king himself might have been the chief rainmaker or at least presided over the rituals. This intertwining of kingship and spiritual stewardship created a leadership model where political stability and environmental harmony were deeply connected. When the rains failed, it pointed to a crisis of legitimacy.

Of course, agriculture was not the only source of wealth and success in Great Zimbabwe. Trade was also important. The city was a key connecting point in the vast regional trade network. From the inland regions of southern Africa, especially in areas known for their gold, like the Mutapa territories, to the wealthy coral-walled cities of the Swahili coast, like Kilwa, Mombasa, and Sofala, all goods had to pass through Great Zimbabwe's hands. The city's role as a major trade center contributed to its influence that rippled across the known world. Persian glassware, Chinese porcelain, and Arab coins were some of the artifacts that have been unearthed by archaeologists, which clearly proved how far Great Zimbabwe's influence stretched.

And yet, for all its outward wealth, Great Zimbabwe's strength lay in its internal cohesion. Families paid tribute, and local leaders maintained allegiance to the capital. The king's court, which is safe for us to assume was composed of advisors, ritualists, and trade overseers, ensured both divine favor and political order.

The "Rediscovery" of Great Zimbabwe

Great Zimbabwe entered a period of decline in the mid-15th century, and it was eventually forgotten by the world by 1450. Indeed, locals never forgot the city. Oral traditions endured that spoke of sacred kings and courts. However, when European explorers stumbled upon the ruins of the city in the 19th century, a controversy soon arose. The early colonial narratives dismissed the idea that Great Zimbabwe was founded by the blood, sweat, and tears of Africans. Even if they had governed the city many centuries earlier, the structures, the Europeans claimed, must have been the work of foreigners. Perhaps the foundations were laid by the Arabs or even the Phoenicians. These theories, steeped in racial bias, persisted for decades, clouding historical inquiry and undermining African achievement.

It was not until 1929 that this view began to fade. British archaeologist Getrude Caton-Thompson led a rigorous excavation in the area. Apart from having worked with a team that included Africans, Gertrude also used stratigraphy to prove that the materials found at Great Zimbabwe, such as local pottery and building remains, were clearly associated with Bantu-speaking peoples. Through this finding, her verdict was clear. Great Zimbabwe was indeed an African creation.

Today, the ruins are protected as a UNESCO World Heritage Site. Visitors, be they avid history lovers or tourists, can walk among the stone walls, inspecting and imagining what life in the city was like many centuries ago. Although the city had long been abandoned, for archaeologists and historians, the site is still very much alive.

Modern archaeology has given us glimpses of the city in its former glory. Carbon dating, soil analysis, and artifact mapping have helped build a picture of daily life, trade, and architecture. Yet, they still cannot answer many questions. Without texts or inscriptions, historians must rely strictly on artifacts, oral traditions, and architectural patterns to reconstruct the past.

Plausible Origins and Debates

While archaeologists now agree that the city was built by Africans, the deeper question remains: which African hands exactly? Many scholars suggest that the founders of the city were the Shona-speaking peoples, particularly those associated with the Gokomere and Leopard's Kopje cultures. These early societies called the region their home from the 9th century to the 13th century.

The Mapungubwe (c. 1075–1220 CE) also could have built it. With the cultural and architectural parallels between Mapungubwe and Great Zimbabwe, including the use of stone walls, dry stone masonry, and hilltop elite enclosures, this earlier stone-walled settlement to the south is believed by many to be the precursor to Great Zimbabwe. Although this suggestion has never been confirmed, many scholars believe there is some degree of continuity or cultural inheritance, especially since the decline of Mapungubwe coincided with the rise of Great Zimbabwe.

But the roots go even deeper. Before the Bantu migrations and the rise of Iron Age societies, the land was home to the San, hunter-gatherer communities that were popular for their rock art. This sparked another mystery. Did the spiritual beliefs and environmental knowledge of the San survive within the later Shona traditions? Some anthropologists think so. The reverence for sacred hills, the role of spirit mediums, and the belief in ancestral intercession may have older echoes than we realize.

Some also questioned the city's political makeup. While some are certain that it was a centralized monarchy led by a divine king whose authority could be felt far into the interior and toward the coast, there are other theories. They propose a more decentralized structure, suggesting that Great Zimbabwe might have even been the ceremonial and economic center of a confederation of elite lineages or semiautonomous communities. It is plausible that they were bound together through tribute, marriage alliances, and shared religious practices.

Unfortunately, this debate cannot be settled easily; the lack of written records complicates coming to a firm conclusion. However, the scale of construction (especially the Hill Complex and the Great Enclosure), the diversity of imported goods, and the city's influence across the continent and beyond suggest a layered political system that was both sophisticated and adaptive.

Being a kingdom that left behind no written records, it is not a surprise that local communities passed down the story of the city through the art of storytelling, songs, and rituals. While some told of a great city once ruled by a monarch with divine powers, others spoke of a sacred oracle who lived in the Hill Complex. There were also tales that served as a warning not to disturb certain sites, as bad luck would befall those who did so. Although these stories were, more often than not, woven in myths and legends, they were passed down as a means to preserve the kingdom's memory.

A copy of a Zimbabwe soapstone bird sculpture.[18]

Perhaps one of the most intriguing mysteries surrounding the city was the Zimbabwe Bird, a stylized soapstone sculpture complete with a hooked beak. In the late 19th century, archaeologists uncovered eight of these sculptures within the ruins of Great Zimbabwe. Scholars were sure that these sculptures were originally placed atop monoliths within the Great Enclosure and Hill Complex. What they were not sure of was the exact meaning or purpose of the sculptures. Were they used as totems of royal lineages or emblems of spiritual guardianship? Perhaps the sculptures served as markers of shrines and were used for communication with their ancestors. No one can confidently arrive at a conclusion, but scholars and historians agree that this image was important. Today, the bird appears on Zimbabwe's national flag.

The flag of Zimbabwe, featuring the Zimbabwe Bird.[19]

Another feature of Great Zimbabwe that puzzled many was its openness. Despite its monumental influence back then and the size of the city, Great Zimbabwe interestingly lacks fortifications. No moats, towers, or any sort of defensive walls were built to keep their enemies, if any, at bay. This led historians to believe that the city enjoyed a period of internal stability. It is plausible that they experienced only minor threats from external forces, or perhaps the city's prestige and ritual authority outweighed military dominance in maintaining power.

Great Zimbabwe might have been home to as many as twenty thousand people at its height. This was indeed a remarkable number, especially for a city that had no riverside farmland or massive irrigation system. Unfortunately, by the mid-15th century, the city saw a decrease in its population. Over time, its markets fell silent, and its pathways, once filled with people, were conquered by weeds.

The reasons for its abandonment remain shrouded in mystery. No conqueror breached the city and razed it to the ground. No plague is known to have swept through the population. There are, of course, theories, though none are definitive.

Environmental strain is one of the most cited. With the city's population tremendously growing, the demand for resources would have surged. Its surrounding region might have suffered from overgrazing and deforestation. Without firewood, construction materials, or grazing lands for cattle, life in the hilltop city would have grown increasingly unsustainable. Combined with water shortages, especially in the dry season, the large population might have found it extremely difficult to continue living within the stone walls of Great Zimbabwe.

Other scholars pointed to trade dynamics. As the Swahili coast grew wealthier and new centers like Sofala rose in prominence, the routes connecting inland goldfields to the coast might have shifted. Over the years, Great Zimbabwe began to lose its monopoly on long-distance trade. And so, without a flourishing trade, the city began to see a decrease in its wealth. Internal politics also might have been the catalyst for its mysterious decline. Without written records, though, it is impossible to confirm if the royal line suffered any fracture. However, it is plausible that the ruling class never succumbed to their fate but rather moved on to seek fresher lands and new trade opportunities. This elite migration is hinted at in the sudden emergence of successor states like Khami and Mutapa, which carried architectural and cultural continuities.

Regardless of the reasons, it is safe to conclude that the city never experienced conquest or catastrophe. It was relinquished and later surrendered to Mother Nature until its story resurfaced again centuries later.

Beyond Zimbabwe: Other Significant Lost Cities

Great Zimbabwe was not the only city that thrived in southern Africa. Across the region, scattered through river valleys and highland ridges, were a few other cities that left their mark. Mapungubwe was one of them. Nestled quietly in the Limpopo Valley (near the modern-day borders of Zimbabwe, South Africa, and Botswana), this settlement was well known to local societies and foreigners, especially in the 11th and 13th centuries. Their influence was born well before Great Zimbabwe reached its peak.

Mapungubwe shared similarities with its more famous cousin, Great Zimbabwe, in terms of social stratification. In Mapungubwe, the elite lived atop the hill, where they were separated from the commoners who lived below. Royal burials here have yielded some of southern Africa's most iconic artifacts, with the small gold rhinoceros being the most popular. Discovered in the 19th century, this particular artifact was delicately crafted from wood and wrapped with sheets of gold, signifying the city's wealth.

The golden rhinoceros of Mapungubwe.[30]

Another one of Mapungubwe's similarities with Zimbabwe lay in its control of trade between inland producers and coastal merchants. Archaeologists unearthed various artifacts in the settlement, which proved how Mapungubwe once accepted visitors from all around the world. However, Mapungubwe was not meant to survive the test of time. By the late 13th century, its name was no longer spoken as it once had been.

Gold beads and jewelry found at Mapungubwe.[21]

Like Great Zimbabwe, its gradual decline was attributed to a combination of several factors. However, it was in 1300 that the settlement found itself closer to decline. Climate change occurred during this period, which saw a shift toward drier and cooler temperatures. This undoubtedly impacted Mapungubwe's agricultural productivity. With resources greatly dwindling, the settlement could no longer support its population. Its cultural legacy, however, did not vanish. Many scholars believe that the elites who once ruled Mapungubwe helped shape the rise of Great Zimbabwe.

Khami was a power that rose in the southwest as Great Zimbabwe faded in the 15th century. Situated near present-day Bulawayo, Khami was best known for its architectural wonders, which were seen by many as a continuity of Great Zimbabwe. Its builders refined the dry stone technique used at Great Zimbabwe, crafting longer walls with more intricate decorative motifs. Checkered and herringbone patterns were common, and unlike Zimbabwe's massive enclosures, Khami's buildings were more linear and terraced.

Khami also showed signs of a more stratified society, perhaps influenced by internal developments and growing contact with

Portuguese traders on the coast. Again, the discovery of imported ceramics, glassware, and gunflints showed the city's increasing connections with the outside world. But still, Khami faced a fate similar to that of its neighbors. By the mid-17th century, the city faced decline as newer polities and shifting alliances altered the political landscape.

The same could be said of Thulamela, a city in the lush regions of present-day Kruger National Park. Flourishing sometime around 1450, this particular walled hilltop settlement was associated with the Zimbabwe culture. It contained elite burials and evidence of sophisticated craftsmanship. Though less extensive than both Great Zimbabwe and Khami, it served as an important regional center until its eventual collapse around 1700.

Stonework is not the only thing that ties all of these cities together. They all shared cultural and technological practices, likely tied to Shona-speaking peoples. These settlements also had the same tradition of leadership that blurred the line between political authority and sacred duty. Indeed, each city rose at a different moment, adapting to the needs and pressures of its time. Yet, all of them reflected a legacy of complex statecraft, long-distance trade, and social stratification well before the arrival of colonial powers.

Chapter 6 – Berber and Moors: The Untold Legacy of North African Dynasties

To many, Tiaret is a major city in northwestern Algeria, nestled beautifully in the scenic Atlas Mountains. To a few others, including the 13th-century historian Ibn Idhari al-Marrakushi, Tiaret was a place of important history. The ancient city's name appears only briefly in his writings. It is often tucked between entries about battles and treaties, but he never dismissed the prominence of Tiaret (also known as Tahert).

Little is known about the historian, but we can safely assume that Ibn Idhari never walked its streets. By the time he wrote his famous book, *al-Bayan al-Mughrib*, the city had already fallen into decline. However, his writings, which contained information he gathered from older texts and travelers' stories, give modern scholars insights into stories of the Berbers' greatness. The Almoravids, the Almohads, and even the Zirids were not just typical dynasties that simply rose and fell. His words, along with those from contemporaries like Ibn Khaldun and al-Bakri, allowed scholars and historians to reimagine the broader story of the Maghreb.

Among the earliest of those Berber dynasties were the Rustamids. Their story began in Tiaret. It was founded by Abd al-Rahman ibn Rustam sometime in the late 8th century. Interestingly, Abd al-Rahman was a leader who embraced the teachings of Ibadi Islam (a sect that was neither Sunni nor Shi'a). This particular school was known for its moderation, egalitarian ideals, and emphasis on justice and consultation.

It made sense for Tiaret to be modest under the Rustamids; there were no golden palaces, and the leaders lived and dressed modestly since they ruled by moral authority. The city was located far from the rest of the imperial capitals, yet it still thrived. Tiaret was once a center of trade and philosophy.

However, the teachings of Ibadi Islam were mostly rejected by the dominant powers at the time, especially the Fatimids of Egypt. When they came sweeping through North Africa in the early 10th century, the Fatimids aimed to do more than just conquer. They wished to crush rival doctrines and impose Shi'a rule. Unfortunately, the Rustamids had little defense, so they could not hold their ground against the advancing Fatimids. Their city eventually fell in 969 CE. The last ruler of the Rustamid dynasty was said to have fled south, bringing with him what remained of his people and what few books they could carry. Some suggest they made it to the M'zab Valley, where Ibadi communities survive to this day. They practiced and preserved the same values but did so quietly.

Of course, Ibn Idhari could not preserve everything in his work. But he left enough for us to remember that the Moors were not merely conquerors and that the Berbers were more than just tribes. He described the crossing of Tariq ibn Ziyad into Iberia in 711 CE, but the historian did not just praise the general's boldness. The Berber soldiers who filled Tariq's ranks were also crucial to the success of this campaign. These men were drawn from the Zenata and Sanhaja tribes. Arabic was not their first language, yet they followed Islam, though they often practiced Islamic customs that were mixed with their tribal traditions. Although their roles were often overshadowed by stories of their leaders and commanders, it is hard to dismiss that they were the ones who formed the backbone of the army that relentlessly marched across the rocky outcrop known as Gibraltar (Jabal Tariq).

The story goes that upon his arrival, Tariq burned the ships that had ferried them across. He then turned to his men and uttered his famous speech, "The enemy is before you, and the sea is behind you. You have no escape but in courage and perseverance."

While the speech might have been dramatized in later chronicles such as the 17th-century *Nafh al-Tib* (authored by al-Maqqari), Tariq's words captured the spirit of what the Berbers were facing. They were embarking on a campaign deep into lands they were unfamiliar with and against the powerful Visigothic kingdom that had long ruled Hispania.

The Berber forces under Tariq, which are estimated to have numbered around seven thousand, met the forces of the last Visigothic king, Roderic, at the Battle of Guadalete. The Islamic Berber forces emerged victorious, and Roderic was said to have died in battle. Almost overnight, the Visigothic command structure crumbled. Cities in the region soon fell with little resistance. Even Toledo, the Visigothic capital, opened its gates to the Berber invaders, followed by Córdoba and Seville. In just a few years, much of the Iberian Peninsula was under Muslim control.

A painting depicting the retreat of Roderic's forces at the Battle of Guadalete.²²

From here on, the world was introduced to the establishment of al-Andalus. It was initially governed by the Umayyad dynasty, whose seat was in Damascus. Under its watchful gaze, al-Andalus bloomed, developing its own administrative centers and military outposts. Although Arab governors from the east held power over the region, they relied heavily on the Berber troops who had won the land in the first place. They knew that without them, success would remain out of reach. However, they were not rewarded equally.

Ibn Khaldun wrote about how the Berber fighters were seen by the Arabs as second-class citizens within the new order of al-Andalus. While the Arab governors were given the richest lands, the Berbers were sent away to frontier zones, far from Córdoba's polished courts. However, the Berbers were not ones to remain idle. In the northern reaches of al-Andalus, the Arab presence was thin, which allowed the Berbers to build and strengthen their own communities. When they sensed the weakening central rule, they immediately seized the chance to act more independently. The Berbers refused to send taxes to Córdoba but instead collected them for their own use. They made their own treaties and passed down power within their families. Their identities slowly transformed from tribal to dynastic.

Meanwhile, back across the strait, the situation in Maghreb was changing. The Umayyad rule was beginning to fracture, leading to the birth of local dynasties driven by both politics and beliefs. New leaders rose who believed that the Arab-led empires had strayed from the faith. These men would go the distance; they did not simply rebel, but they aimed to build an empire. The age of the Berber dynasties was about to begin. The Berbers were eager to leave their marks not only on Africa and Spain but also on Europe itself.

The Almoravid Dynasty

Marrakesh did not yet exist when Yusuf ibn Tashfin first arrived on the plains of southern Morocco. The area was nothing more than just open land with dry winds constantly blowing and various tribes either reaching yet another peace treaty or preparing for battle. Yusuf, however, knew the region was full of potential. He aimed not to just conquer but also unite the scattered tribes under Allah and law.

Yusuf ibn Tashfin was used to the harsh desert life. He was a leader of the Lamtuna, one of the Sanhaja Berber tribes that were loyal to a strict interpretation of Islam. Yusuf was also a follower of Abdallah ibn Yasin, a reformer whose doctrine called for religious renewal among the Berbers of the Sahara. It was from Abdallah's teachings that the Almoravid movement was born.

By 1056, this movement transformed into a state. With Yusuf at the forefront, the Almoravids were able to conquer neighboring tribes and towns. They then began spreading their message of religious discipline and political unity. It was only around 1070 that the Almoravid dynasty was formally established. Yusuf next turned his attention to building a center for the new dynasty. And so, Marrakesh was founded.

The city was well planned and fortified. It was a symbol of Almoravid rule. Its water channels, bustling markets, and grand mosques gave the city both spiritual and administrative importance.

Yusuf soon planned to extend his empire. He fixed his eyes on the regions across modern-day Morocco and western Algeria. His mission was simple: he wanted to create a disciplined empire rooted in Maliki Islam and Berber leadership.

Of course, with more territories secured, Yusuf grew more ambitious. His attention turned northward, where al-Andalus still stood. The golden opportunity for Yusuf to present his influence came in 1086. The Muslim taifa kings of a fragmented and weakened Iberia had summoned his help. (Taifas were independent Muslim kingdoms and principalities in the Iberian Peninsula.) They faced relentless attacks from the Christian Kingdom of León and Castile. Led by King Alfonso VI, the Christians had successfully taken Toledo. Afraid that they would soon face complete defeat, the taifa rulers gave Yusuf the responsibility of defending their land.

Without hesitation, Yusuf and his forces, which were largely composed of Berber cavalry, crossed the Strait of Gibraltar, eventually facing Alfonso's army at the Battle of Sagrajas. Yusuf achieved a major victory when the Berbers delivered a crushing blow to the Christian forces. However, this was not the last time that Yusuf would set foot in al-Andalus. After all, he had seen firsthand the weakness of the taifa rulers.

Despite having room to breathe once more, the taifa did not use this opportunity for renewed defense. In fact, many returned to their old rivalries and indulgences. They even exacted taxes that burdened their people. There were also those who resumed paying tribute (known as parias) to the Christian kings. All of this was witnessed by Yusuf himself, who returned to al-Andalus multiple times in the years following his victorious battle. By 1090, the Almoravids could no longer stand and watch as the taifa kings turned into unfit protectors of Islam. He chose to take action and assert his dominance.

Yusuf eventually managed to secure approval of his mission from the Abbasid caliph in Baghdad. He was given legitimacy as a true defender of the faith. With this support, Yusuf wasted no time in deposing many of the taifa rulers. He strongly believed that the moral and military survival of al-Andalus depended on stronger and unified leadership, which he could offer.

From here on, al-Andalus was incorporated into the Almoravid Empire, followed by Córdoba, Seville, and Badajoz. These cities were brought under tighter religious and political control. Of course, this change of hands was not accepted by everyone. Andalusian elites especially resented the Almoravids' simplicity and strict orthodoxy. Tensions began to simmer underneath the surface between Berber troops and the more refined Andalusian society.

Still, Yusuf ruled for over four decades, finally meeting his demise in 1106. Despite his power, Yusuf dressed simply, ate modestly, and often refused flattery. Even historian al-Bakri described Yusuf as a ruler without ornament but full of resolve.

Following his death, the throne was passed to his son, Ali ibn Yusuf. In contrast to his father, Ali was born in a palace surrounded by scholars and luxury. However, the new Almoravid ruler was still considered a capable ruler, though his name was not always remembered in history books like his father's. Under his reign, Marrakesh's defenses saw great improvements. New irrigation systems were introduced. Ali also contributed to the expansion of the Great Mosque of Tlemcen, which still stands to this day.

The Great Mosque of Tlemcen today.[20]

Known for his devoutness and patronage of learning and the arts, it is not surprising that Ali brought more mathematicians and jurists into his court. He also played a hand in expanding the Almoravids' geographical extent.

Unfortunately, despite being a capable ruler, the empire witnessed early signs of decline under his reign. Cities in the east that were once loyal to the Almoravids began to break away. In the west, tribes that had once spoken highly about Yusuf grew impatient.

Then, news arrived during the later years of Ali's rule that spoke about a new movement in the mountains of the High Atlas. It began with a preacher named Ibn Tumart, who had long been frustrated with the state of Islam under the Almoravids. As his followers grew, so did his voice. Ibn Tumart was said to have condemned the Almoravids as hypocrites. The Almohads, which they soon became known as, would be the contender to the Almoravid dynasty.

The Almohad Dynasty

The path to Tinmel was not an easy walk in the park. It was high in the Atlas Mountains, and the road was both narrow and treacherous. Only a few dared to climb it. One of them was \ Ibn Tumart, who turned Tinmel into the very heart of a revolution.

Ibn Tumart was not a soldier by training. Belonging to a Masmuda Berber family near Sous, he was very familiar with the Eastern Islamic world. Having studied in Mecca, Baghdad, and possibly Damascus, Ibn Tumart came home with a deep understanding of theology and philosophy. The preacher saw the need for change. He was deeply disturbed by the constant sight of rulers indulging in luxury while the scholars remained silent. He could not stand still while faith was becoming a thing of the past.

The Maliki school is one of the four major Sunni schools of Islamic law. It emphasizes tradition and local consensus, which allowed for some integration of local Berber customs. While the Almoravids believed this school was crucial for bringing order and orthodoxy to the empire, Ibn Tumart saw things differently. He opposed it—and in extension, the Almoravids—since many of the local customs that had blended with the faith were rather un-Islamic. He also saw the Maliki approach as rigid, overly literal, and blind to the deeper truths of monotheism (*tawḥīd*).

When he preached in markets and mosques, Ibn Tumart called for strict adherence to the Qur'an and hadith (the Islamic oral tradition of the Prophet Muhammad). He publicly rejected the Almoravids' tolerance. He gathered supporters from his preachings here, but things took a darker turn after he challenged an Almoravid judge in Marrakesh. The Almoravids, who were known to often suppress other viewpoints, expelled the preacher. This was when he retreated into the High Atlas, eventually forming the Almohad movement.

When he finally had the numbers—Ibn Tumart had support from various Berber tribes, particularly the Masmuda—the Almohads launched their move. They met the Almoravid forces in 1130 at the Battle of al-Buhayra. Despite enjoying an early success, the Almohads failed to topple their enemy. Many died during the conflict. Ibn Tumart survived, but he died a few months later.

For seventeen years, the Almoravid dynasty was able to enjoy some peace. However, his death did not extinguish the fire. The mantle was passed to Abd al-Mu'min. Known to be a loyal follower of Ibn Tumart and a capable leader, he successfully unified the Berber tribes under the Almohad banner. In 1147, Marrakesh finally fell and, with it, the last of the Almoravids.

With Abd al-Mu'min as the new caliph, the Almohads expanded their empire, covering Libya up to the Atlantic and into Iberia. With these territories firmly in its grasp, the Almohad caliphate knew it was time to centralize power and issue legal reforms. Instead of tribal favoritism, the Almohads prioritized meritocracy. Arabic was promoted, but the dynasty never erased its Berber identity; this remained strong, especially in rural administration.

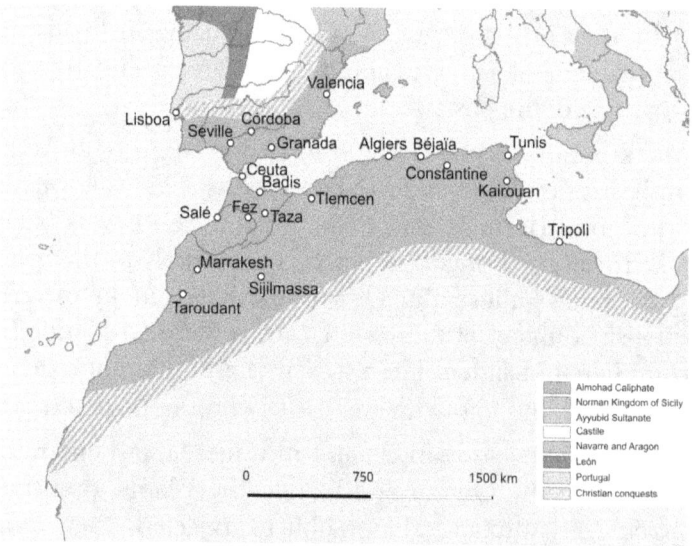

The territories under the Almohad dynasty.[34]

64

The Almohads also left behind some of the greatest architectural achievements of medieval Islam. The Giralda Tower in Seville, for instance, was an impressive structure. With its precise geometric design and spiraling ramps, it is amazing to think that the tower once called Muslims to prayer before transforming into the bell tower of a Christian cathedral years later. The Koutoubia Mosque in Marrakesh and the Hassan Tower in Rabat were also architectural contributions of the Almohads.

In contrast to the Almoravids, the Almohads encouraged philosophical and scientific inquiry, as long as it supported their vision of unity and divine order. This can clearly be seen when Abu Yaqub Yusuf became the second Almohad caliph. He was known to have acknowledged and supported the work of many scholars. One of them was Ibn Tufayl, the Arab Andalusian Muslim philosopher who authored the first philosophical novel, *Hayy ibn Yaqzan*. Many of those familiar with philosophy today agree that this Arabic novel was the precursor to the 18th-century book *Robinson Crusoe*. Another scholar was Ibn Rushd (Averroes), the great philosopher whose commentaries on Aristotle would later fuel debate in both the Islamic world and medieval Europe.

Their works reflected the Almohad belief that reason and revelation could walk together, even if they sometimes disagreed. However, it is unfair to assume that the Almohad doctrine was always peaceful. More often than not, the Almohads were hostile to those who did not accept their faith. Non-Muslims were usually forced to convert, and heretical thought was not tolerated outside court circles. There were times when scholars were silenced when their ideas reached too far.

Of course, like its predecessor, the Almohad dynasty was never meant to taste glory for too long. While Abu Yusuf Ya'qub al-Mansur reigned, the Almohads were able to achieve great victories, such as the Battle of Alarcos in 1195. However, these victories failed to build lasting peace. Troubles still brewed in both North Africa and Iberia, as the people there were discontent with the Almohad dynasty's strict rule. Over time, the dynasty saw a period where tribal alliances frayed. Andalusian cities began slipping from its grasp.

A painting depicting the Battle of Las Navas de Tolosa.[25]

It did not help that the Almohads suffered a crushing defeat in 1212 at the hands of the Christian Reconquista. True, the dynasty continued to survive following the Battle of Las Navas de Tolosa, but they were only around for a few more decades. Eventually, the dynasty's strength broke, and more rivals rose across the Maghreb, eager to challenge the Almohads' authority. The dynasty came to an end by the mid-13th century. This was when the Almohads lost control of their most precious jewel, Marrakesh, to yet another Berber Muslim dynasty known as the Marinids. The ruling caliph at the time, Idris al-Wathiq, was captured and later executed.

The Zirid Dynasty, Rulers of Kairouan

The roots of the Zirid dynasty could be traced back as early as the 10th century. It was founded by Buluggin ibn Ziri, a Sanhaja Berber. The Zirids were best known for being loyal vassals of the Fatimid Caliphate—at least for a while. They had a relatively good relationship, to the point where they were entrusted with governing Ifriqiya (roughly modern-day Tunisia and eastern Algeria) on behalf of their Shi'a overlords in Egypt. This gave way for the Fatimids to strengthen their defenses at Cairo and expand their influence into the Levant while the Zirids oversaw local rule, trade, and defense.

This relationship, however, would soon change. As the Fatimids drifted deeper into religious ideology and Eastern politics, the Zirids grew more confident and rooted in their own lands. Their culture blended Berber traditions with Arab-Islamic scholarship. Kairouan began to flourish. Farmers brought in harvests from their irrigated fields, while scholars flocked into the city to teach law, astronomy, and medicine. Coastal cities like Mahdia also bustled with trade across the Mediterranean.

The major turning point came when the Zirids saw the rise of their fourth ruler, al-Mu'izz ibn Badis. A devout Sunni Muslim, al-Mu'izz was not afraid to publicly reject the authority of the Fatimid caliph. Upon finally ending the decades of allegiance to the Shi'a regime, he moved to recognize the Sunni Abbasid caliph in Baghdad. While some view this move as nothing more than just a theological break, others thought of it as a political strategy. Through this, al-Mu'izz stated his state was independent and claimed sovereignty.

The Fatimids were undoubtedly enraged with this outcome, yet they did not retaliate with an army. Instead, they dispatched tribes to wreak havoc in Zirid territory. Waves of Bedouin nomads were sent, especially those who had been growing restless in Upper Egypt. Eager to punish the Zirids and solve a domestic problem at the same time, the Fatimids unleashed them on Ifriqiya like a human flood.

Al-Mu'izz was said to have underestimated the threat at first, but it did not take long for him to see the consequences. Known as the Hilalian invasion (named after the tribes of Bani Hilal), this movement of tribes included men, women, children, and even animals. They crossed the desert with speed and violence. Crops were burned, and cities were razed and looted. The sophisticated irrigation networks that once ensured the smooth flow of resources in the region were dismantled. Kairouan, the jewel of both North Africa and the Zirids themselves, was eventually sacked in 1057. Its libraries were trampled upon and its countryside disturbed.

Al-Mu'izz was not so easily deterred. He retreated to the coastal city of Mahdia (located on the eastern coast of modern Tunisia). Fortunately, the city was already fortified, thanks to the Fatimids, who developed it and made it their capital city a century prior. Here, the Zirids tried to continue their legacy. Mahdia was a strategic refuge. It offered more defense from inland enemies like the Bani Hilal and was well connected to the Mediterranean trade. However, the Zirids could never mirror their old success.

The city had to rely on maritime commerce and piracy. While these activities kept it afloat, the Zirids eventually found themselves diplomatically isolated. This and the increase in European naval raids led the Zirids to realize they were nearing the end of the line. By 1148, the Zirids had lost Mahdia to the Normans. Although the port city continued to thrive under various rulers, the Zirid dynasty was no more.

Chapter 7 – Treasures of the Swahili Coast: Secrets of the Indian Ocean Trade

When people hear the name Indian Ocean, many cannot help but imagine an endless stretch of water. While some picture an image of calm blue waves with no land in sight, there are also those who conjure images of mysterious creatures swimming deep below the surface or perhaps the wreckage of ancient ships that found its home on the seabed many meters down. However, believe it or not, in the past, this ocean was far from empty. It was full of life—and we are not talking about sea creatures.

For many centuries, the Indian Ocean had been one of the busiest trade routes in the world. Long before the Atlantic became the center of global travel and shipping, the Indian Ocean connected Africa, Arabia, Persia, India, and even Southeast Asia. The ocean was a moving highway. During the medieval period, the water was filled with ships carrying an array of goods like gold, ivory, spices, and exquisite cloth and silk. Of course, these goods were not the only things that ships carried across this ocean. Travelers also brought ideas, languages, and religions.

One such merchant—let us call him Yusuf—went on multiple journeys across the Indian Ocean, ending up in several African coastal cities. He hailed from the port city of Hormuz, located at the edge of Persia. Yusuf's father was also a trader. His father often told him stories of his travels, and his favorite were about the cities along the Swahili coast. His father spoke highly of these eastern African trade ports.

"I will never forget the sight of the stone houses and crowded markets," Yusuf's father may have said to his son. "And the sweet scent of spices that hung in the air."

When Yusuf reached adulthood, he became a merchant. He sailed to every port city along the Arabian Peninsula. He knew he had to see the coastal cities of East Africa next. So, he bid farewell to his small family of three and embarked on a journey. Yusuf timed his voyage carefully. The monsoon winds, which blew southward between November and March, were now at his back. Unlike the unpredictable currents of the Atlantic, the Indian Ocean offered sailors a kind of rhythm. These seasonal winds blew in one direction for half the year and then reversed. This natural rhythm allowed merchants and travelers to plan their voyage precisely. They could disembark from Hormuz and head to the East African coast in one season, do their business there, and return home when the wind changed direction a few months later.

Yusuf looked over the goods stored in his hold. In one crate were glass beads he had gotten from India, while another had bright cotton cloth that originated from Gujarat. He also had a small chest of cloves and several rolls of Persian silk. He had brought these as gifts and payments. Once he arrived at his destination, Yusuf planned to trade these goods for gold, ivory tusks, animal hides, rare hardwoods, and resins used in incense.

Yusuf also carried letters written by his merchant friends in Hormuz and scholars. They were to be delivered to contacts along the Swahili coast. He knew that the Indian Ocean trade was not strictly about buying and selling items but also about building trust and relationships. Traders like himself were part of a wider web of people who shared languages, religion, and customs, even though they came from different shores. He knew that trade was one of the ways of gaining knowledge.

"Once you reach the Swahili coast, remember to listen more than you speak," he recalled what his father had told him. "Their cities are older than your maps. Their people are well-versed in their surroundings. They know the sea as well as the stars."

After weeks of sailing the ocean, Yusuf could finally spot land. His face brightened as his ship drew closer to shore. He could see high walls rising above the waterline. Yusuf had arrived at Kilwa, one of the coastal

Swahili port cities that his father once spoke of. This was no small trading post. Near the harbor, dozens of wooden dhows (a type of trading vessel) were preparing to dock. Yusuf could see merchants unloading baskets of dates and nuts. Some men were loading their ships with ivory tusks and fine cloth, preparing to leave. On one side, women walked around with baskets of herbs and dyed cloth balanced on their heads.

A Yemeni stamp with an illustration of a dhow, a vessel typically used by merchants.[36]

Kilwa was undoubtedly laden with wealth. After all, the city controlled trade with the African interior. Precious goods like gold, iron, and even slaves passed through this port. These goods were then transported north by sea to Arabia and Persia. Much of the gold came through Sofala, another port farther south, where goods from Great Zimbabwe were brought to the coast. Kilwa had once conquered Sofala to control that trade. Now, nearly all the gold passing through the Swahili coast flowed through Kilwa's hands.

A 16th century depiction of Kilwa.[37]

The ruins of Kilwa today.[38]

Yusuf was eager to explore Kilwa. He followed the sounds of the market, which led him to a wide yet packed street lined with coral-stone buildings—just like what his father had described. A few houses caught his attention; they had imported Chinese porcelain set into their walls, acting like shining ornaments. Kilwa obviously had visitors from as far as East Asia. Yusuf also saw the Great Mosque of Kilwa, which stood at the center of the city. At that time, the structure was considered one of the largest mosques in sub-Saharan Africa. Though what remains of the mosque today are mostly ruins, at its height, the structure was topped with a great dome, and its interior was filled with beautiful arches.

What remains of the interior of Kilwa's Great Mosque.[29]

During his stay, Yusuf learned a little bit about Sultan al-Hasan ibn Sulaiman. He ruled Kilwa when it was at its peak in the 14th century. The sultan also contributed to the expansion of the city. He commissioned various construction projects, including the Palace of Husuni Kubwa, which overlooked the Indian Ocean. Everyone who laid eyes on the palace was said to have left with complete awe. It once boasted a hundred rooms, an octagonal swimming pool, and a staging area for loading and unloading goods from a ship. Knowing that trade was Kilwa's beating heart, the sultan made sure to welcome every trader from across the ocean with open arms. Power was almost perfectly balanced under his reign, and Kilwa was able to enjoy a period of peace and wealth.

Wealth was not the only thing that mattered here. Yusuf noticed that Islam was central to daily life. The call to prayer echoed from the minarets five times a day. Locals and Muslim foreigners like himself would pause their activities to pray. Children studied Arabic and memorized verses from the Quran. The widespread Islamic practices here were not a surprise; Kilwa had been founded by settlers who hailed from Arabia and Persia. The Swahili oral traditions and other sources, like the *Kilwa Chronicle*, mentioned that the city was the brainchild of a Persian prince named Ali ibn al-Hassan Shirazi. It was believed that he built the city after purchasing the island from a local Bantu-speaking chief. However, despite being founded by an outsider, Kilwa never lost its culture and tradition. Instead, the locals fused influences from both Arabia and Persia into their own local customs.

Yusuf remained in Kilwa for a few weeks before setting sail again. This time, he headed north along the Swahili coast. Perhaps luck was on his side, as the journey was not perilous. His ship followed the familiar curve of the land. He passed the green shorelines and narrow inlets while stopping at a few fishing villages along the way. The monsoon wind was steady, and the sea was very calm, allowing our merchant to arrive at his next stop, the port city of Mombasa, without any incident.

Mombasa may attract tourists with its safari adventures and exceptional beaches today, but in Yusuf's time, visitors flocked there for trade and commerce. Traders and merchants liked to stop here because of its well-protected harbor. Yusuf could see ships from the southern coast of Africa, Arabia, and even India bobbing in the distance. Almost similar to Kilwa, the streets of Mombasa were lined with a series of buildings made of coral stone. If it were not for the tall palm trees, Yusuf would not be able to fully open his eyes, as the sun was scorching.

In contrast to Kilwa, Mombasa was not only known for trade. It was also known for its exquisite craftsmanship. The city was a melting pot of builders and metalworkers. Day and night, Yusuf could hear the sound of hammers hitting anvils. From iron tools typically used to till the land to swords and jewelry, these items were all carefully made and sold to traders from all over the globe.

Yusuf noticed the other goods that constantly flowed through the markets, such as grain, honey, tortoise shells, coconut oil, Indian cotton, and Yemeni incense. Despite the trade at the harbors and markets, business here was orderly. Port officials could be seen exacting their duty. They ensured cargo was taxed and tracked correctly.

Yusuf had a few more stops to make before he could return to his homeland, so he did not linger in Mombasa for too long. After restocking his supplies and trading with the locals for some iron tools and finely made jewelry, he moved on to explore the Zanzibar Archipelago. He sailed farther north until he arrived at the island of Unguja. Even from a distance, he could smell the scent of clove and smoke. Even though cloves would become Zanzibar's main export in later centuries, spices, coconuts, and textiles made the island a vibrant center of trade in Yusuf's time.

Yusuf had a contact here, a local whom he had met a few years back. He invited our merchant to his home, which stood near the busy market. His house appeared modest at first, with thick white walls and a carved wooden door painted in blue. However, when Yusuf stepped inside, he was immediately greeted by a sense of coziness and warmth. The floor was lined with mats, and the brass lamps cast a soft light on the bookshelves. Yusuf knew his friend was a scholar, and he learned more about how Islam had taken root along the Swahili coast. The faith came not through armies or rulers but through families, teachers, and merchants like himself.

He also learned that it was common for children in Zanzibar to speak both Swahili and Arabic. Some, especially those who came from wealth, even pursued education as far away as Hadhramaut or Mecca. What surprised Yusuf the most was the Swahili women. Most women in wealthier households managed trade accounts and were involved in the storage and sale of goods. Islamic law allowed them to inherit and control property; many actually owned the homes in which they lived.

They were also entrusted as guardians of the family's wealth whenever their husbands were away. In Zanzibar and other Swahili coastal cities, their voices were respected. It was not uncommon for them to tend to their shop and supervise their workers during the day and teach the Quran to their children at night.

Yusuf now understood how these coastal cities were part of something larger. Although each had its own set of rulers and customs, they were all somehow tied together by the ocean, faith, trade, and their shared respect for knowledge and hospitality. Yusuf wished he could stay longer, but he had two more destinations to visit.

The monsoon winds carried him farther south, eventually reaching Sofala, located today in Mozambique. He had heard so many things about the city.

"I never set foot in Sofala," Yusuf recalled his father's words. "But from what I heard, the city's wealth did not lie in its streets or towers but in the gold dust carried down the rivers."

Yusuf was unimpressed by what he saw. The city was quieter than Kilwa. The surrounding buildings bore the same coral-stone style, but its harbor was shallow. Ships, including his own, had to anchor at a distance. Only small vessels could maneuver easily. Merchants used these smaller boats to ferry their goods to and from their larger vessels.

It was only when Yusuf stepped into the marketplace that he realized the meaning behind his father's words. Although Sofala was not as vibrant as the other port cities he had visited, traders exchanged goods brought from far inland, as well as from forests, hills, and dry plains— likely from the empire of Great Zimbabwe.

Yusuf met with a local trader who had made the inland journey many times. He told Yusuf of the vast trade network that stretched from the Zambezi River to the highlands. There, people mined gold by hand and shaped the precious nuggets into rings or melted them into bars. These goods then passed from chief to chief before finally arriving at the coast. Although going through these steps took an unimaginable amount of time, the value of gold in Persia and India made the wait worthwhile.

By this point, several months had passed since Yusuf set sail from his homeland. He was ready to return home, but he had one last stop. As his dhow began its return journey northward, he stopped by the southern Somali coast, where the Ajuran Sultanate ruled with a firm hand.

According to other sailors he had met along the way, this place was not often visited by men like him.

"They do not welcome every ship that approaches their harbor. The Ajuran sultans are always careful with whom they trade," one of the sailors told him.

"They control everything," another chimed in. "The water, the roads, and even the scholars. They keep close ties only with local merchants, and high and strict taxes are imposed on foreign traders like you."

Yet, this did not deter Yusuf. He continued his voyage, eventually arriving at Mogadishu, the main port city under the Ajuran Sultanate. From the moment he stepped onto the harbor, Yusuf could see that the sailors he had met were telling the truth. Guards stood at every entrance, eyeing everyone who came and went. Trade officials inspected the cargo with sharp eyes. Merchants spoke in careful tones. Although the people were respectful, they were also reserved, especially with outsiders.

Yusuf realized how the sultanate's power was based on trade alone. Like the sailors told him, the Ajuran Sultanate controlled the waters. Yusuf saw the network of wells and cisterns across the arid interior, which allowed the sultan to manage agriculture and movement through the region. Offending the sultan meant being cut off from water and trade.

The sultanate also had stone fortresses inland. The soldiers were well trained and deeply loyal. Yusuf was told that to avoid conflict, local clans paid tribute to the empire. These clans knew that a single order from the court in Mogadishu could close an entire trade route. Regardless of this strictness, the Ajuran were respected. Their justice system was said to be fair, and the empire's Islamic scholars were known as among the wisest in East Africa. Many had traveled as far as Mecca and returned to Mogadishu with rare books. There were also those who taught in Cairo or exchanged letters with jurists in Arabia. It is safe to say that their legal rulings were trusted and that their governance was admired.

The city of Merca, one of the administrative centers of the Ajuran Sultanate.[80]

Yusuf also met a skilled Somali navigator who was hunched over an old star chart. The navigator explained the unique Somali navigation techniques to Yusuf. He gave new insights into how to read the stars and trace the monsoon winds. The Somali navigator told him that they did not map their journey on drawings alone but also through chants passed down from master to apprentice. These songs spoke of reefs, winds, and landmarks. They were often sung softly at sea to remember when to shift sail or turn toward shore. Although Yusuf was a skilled sailor, this encounter rewarded him with more insight into life at sea.

Yusuf finally returned to Hormuz following his stay in Mogadishu. His ship was laden with all sorts of goods, and his mind was filled with a lot of memories. His crates of glass beads and silks fetched good prices. The gold, ivory, spices, and animal hides he brought home were also met with eager hands. He would return to the Swahili coast years later, but the region would look much different from how he remembered.

While the cities still existed and the coral buildings still stood strong, the mood in the ports had changed. The locals bore a frown on their faces. Above the fortresses, foreign flags flew. In the harbors, Yusuf could only see a few dhows belonging to the merchants. Most of the ships had tall wooden hulls and iron cannons. Yusuf realized that the Portuguese had finally arrived on the coast. It was clear that they did not come just to trade. They had weapons with them, along with maps and their hunger for control.

In 1498, the locals saw the arrival of Vasco da Gama. This marked an era when trade was no longer built on trust and kinship. Instead, it was forced under a system of licenses and tribute. Cities were attacked. Many were looted and forced into submission. While many ports fell to the Portuguese, some tried to resist. However, the European power proved to be relentless. Treaties were reached, but most of them were signed under pressure. Those who refused to cooperate would face bombardment or blockades. Kilwa, for example, was burned, and Mombasa was besieged. Other smaller ports were either absorbed into the Portuguese system or left to fade in isolation.

Chapter 8 – The Lesser-Known Medieval Kingdom of Central Africa

The sails swelled as the Atlantic wind caught hold of them. It pushed the wooden ship further into the mouth of the Congo River. The people on board could sense a different breeze. Compared to where they came from, it was warmer and definitely richer. They could smell the scent of mud from the river, the thick forests nearby, and the salty sea behind them. Suddenly, a man draped in linen stepped out of the cabin. He was a Portuguese captain, and he was eager to finally land in sub-Saharan Africa after months of sailing.

The year was 1483, and the Portuguese believed they had come to claim a new world. Aboard the ship was a scribe who stood beside the mast. In his hands was a leather-bound notebook that he used to record discoveries. Another man held tightly to a crucifix as he whispered prayers for safe passage and successful conversions of the locals. Perhaps to some, these sailors were merely explorers and emissaries sent by a distant king. To others, they were more than that. These people were seeking profit, as they had been sent by the king of Portugal to map coastlines, forge alliances, and open routes to rich goldfields they heard lay inland.

Their mission was clear. The Portuguese were to convert the pagans in this vast land, outmaneuver the Muslim traders who had dominated the region's commerce for centuries, and enrich the royal treasury. However, they had only vague knowledge of what lay ahead. Yes, the Portuguese had better equipment and technology, but what they did not know was that this land was far from empty. The kingdoms scattered throughout the region were not waiting to be discovered. But the Portuguese would not back down easily. One day, they would call them allies, but later, they would call them subjects or rebels.

The Kingdom of Kongo

Long before the arrival of the Portuguese in Central Africa, the Kingdom of Kongo stood tall and proud. Its rulers held control from the forested highlands to the Atlantic shore. Unbeknownst to the European foreigners, Kongo was a centralized and complex state.

Of course, the kingdom was not born overnight. Its roots stretched back to the late 14th century. This was a time when a leader named Lukeni lua Nimi rose to prominence.

A painting of Lukeni lua Nimi based on oral traditions.[81]

Lukeni was said to have hailed from a small chiefdom in the northeast. Eager to unite the Bantu-speaking communities under a single banner, he launched a campaign to conquer neighboring territories around the Kongo River Basin. Using a combination of both conquest and strategic alliances, Lukeni was able to seize control of Mbanza Kongo in the early 1400s. He turned this hilltop settlement into the kingdom's capital. Lukeni worked to build an organized kingdom structured around kingship, tribute, and ritual authority. His descendants would later claim the divine right to rule, linking their lineage not only to great warriors but also to the spirit world itself.

By the early 15th century, Kongo had become a structured kingdom with well-defined provinces. At the top of the political hierarchy stood the manikongo, who acted as the supreme ruler. He did not rule alone; he was supported by a network of nobles who governed territories and collected tributes. The nobles (mani) had to swear loyalty to the king, but they had power of their own. Although it was common for mani to come from long-standing local lineages, the manikongo would also appoint governors from outside kin groups to maintain balance and prevent any family from growing too powerful.

As for the capital, Mbanza Kongo, the city grew into a political and religious center. Stone buildings dotted the area, along with many open courtyards and colorful markets. The kingdom's trade networks were so vast that they stretched inland toward the Atlantic coast. Since Kongo's economy relied on agriculture, fishing, and trade, it was normal to see an abundance of crops and fish in the markets. However, goods like raffia cloth, palm oil, ivory, and copper ingots attracted foreign merchants. These items were also a form of tribute paid to the governors serving under the manikongo.

When the Portuguese ship made an appearance in 1483, the foreigners were welcomed with mixed views. Commanded by the navigator and mariner Diogo Cão, the Portuguese arrived with a smile on their faces. They came bearing gifts and priests to spread the teachings of Christ. Some sources described the Portuguese being somewhat astounded by what they saw. Instead of stepping into the wilderness, they found a kingdom in full command of itself. They were surprised to see a kingdom with a royal court, finely dressed nobles, and an organized society. Still, this did not stop them from claiming new lands and souls.

The foreigners were received by Nzinga a Nkuwu, the ruling manikongo at the time. Fueled by curiosity, the manikongo allowed them to settle. He even took the time to listen to the priests, eventually accepting baptism in 1491 and changing his name to João I. His decision opened the door not just to a new faith but also to diplomatic ties, trade, and influence. However, it was his son, Afonso I (also known as Mbemba a Nzinga), who walked through that door. From a young age, he was educated by missionaries. Afonso was also fluent in Latin.

Over time, he began to believe that Kongo could become a Christian kingdom. Under his reign, Kongo saw the rise of new churches. He also opened schools and encouraged the kingdom to welcome more priests and artisans. The manikongo even made the effort to send delegations to Lisbon, receiving scholars and gifts in return. Of course, Afonso never wished to erase the identity of his people or merely copy Europe. He envisioned a kingdom that could hold onto its African heritage while welcoming European knowledge. He wanted Kongolese Christianity to be shaped by his people's values.

The Baptism of Nzinga a Nkuwu.[32]

Unfortunately, it did not take long for cracks to appear in the relationship between Kongo and the Europeans. The Portuguese soon began to show their true colors. More Portuguese traders arrived on the shores of Kongo, but they sought more than just ivory and gold. Their attention was on slaves. More often than not, they ignored the authority of the manikongo. They struck deals with local leaders or resorted to abducting people outright. Afonso attempted to stop this. He was said to have written a series of letters to the king of Portugal himself. He warned the monarch of the chaos that had been happening in Kongo because of the slave trade. He explained how his state was being terribly depopulated and that even the noblemen were being taken.

The manikongo did everything in his power to mend his kingdom. He asked for a printing press so that Christian texts could be copied in Kikongo and made accessible to everyone. He also asked for a bishop who would serve Kongo instead of Lisbon. Afonso dreamed of a kingdom that could be both African and Catholic. Yet, Portugal's priorities were changing. It was clear that the Europeans were focused on building a stronger coastal presence in southern Central Africa, especially with the growing slave trade in the Atlantic. They even succeeded in founding the port city of Luanda in 1575. This city became a center of slaving operations and colonial expansion. From here, the Portuguese began pushing deeper into Africa more aggressively. They were obviously challenging Kongo's western frontiers.

The situation grew even more dire by the mid-17th century. The Portuguese no longer saw Kongo as a partner. Now more armed and ambitious than ever, the foreigners viewed Kongo as a problem. Tensions simmered in 1665 when Portuguese officials in Luanda laid demands on King António I. The foreigners wanted unrestricted access to slaves. They demanded that the king hand over captives from inland raids and allow Portuguese agents to collect tribute and control key trade routes, especially those connecting the interior to the Atlantic ports. Most importantly of all, they demanded recognition of Portugal's supremacy in the region. The Portuguese sought to turn Kongo into something closer to a vassal state than an equal ally.

When António I refused to surrender local chiefs or bend to colonial authority, tensions escalated. The king knew that yielding to these terms would mean the end of Kongo's sovereignty. So, he rallied other African rulers against Portuguese influence. Some oral traditions suggest he tried to open diplomatic ties with the Dutch. War was in the air.

António led his army in the Battle of Mbwila near the border of Kongo and Angola. This ended badly for Kongo. António was killed, and the Portuguese severed his head, sending it back to Luanda as a symbol of their victory.

Although the Kingdom of Kongo did not disappear overnight, it never returned to its old glory. The central authority had crumbled, setting the path for civil war. Provinces eventually broke away. It was clear that Afonso's dream of a strong Christian African kingdom respected by Europe was going to fade into memory.

The Beginning of the Kingdom of Luba

There was once a man named Kongolo Mwamba. He was a warlord who had risen to power among the broken clans scattered throughout the valleys of southern Central Africa. After conquering neighboring territories, Kongolo began to dream of uniting the people of the Upemba Depression and becoming their supreme ruler. As much as he was a warrior, Kongolo was also a believer. Before setting out on a journey to establish a kingdom, he first sought out words from the prophet Mujibu.

"You may wear the crown," Mujibu said. "But not for long, as you are not of the Bulopwe [the sacred royal blood]."

Kongolo's expression changed, but he listened.

"One day, a man will come to you," Mujibu continued. "If you welcome him, then the kingdom you envisioned will come true, and your name shall live forever. But if you betray him, God will take your power, and your blood shall end in violence."

Kongolo was not content with the prophecy. Regardless, he went on and ruled his people and those he conquered. However, Kongolo was a tyrant. His reign was rather violent.

Sometime later, a man named Ilunga Mbidi left his kingdom far to the east—possibly beyond the shores of Lake Tanganyika—for unknown reasons. While some believed he was guided by a vision, others claimed he was sent by none other than God himself. His journey led him to Kongolo's sisters, Mabela and Bulala. The two women were enthralled by Ilunga. Legend has it that the man bore an appearance that was strikingly different from the people of the Upemba Basin. He was tall, dark-skinned, and had sharp features. He also had a red feather tucked in his hair. Ilunga was also said to have worn a robe that showed his royalty. The sisters immediately recognized him as someone with influence, and they brought Ilunga to their brother's court.

Kongolo received him with curiosity at first. When he finally learned that Ilunga was not just a warrior but also a hunter and a strategist, he began to admire him. Eventually, Kongolo made him the head of his army. Under Ilunga's command, expansion campaigns bore fruit. Through war and diplomacy, the region was successfully unified, finally leading to the establishment of the Kingdom of Luba in 1585.

Perhaps as a reward and to strengthen the ties with Ilunga, Kongolo gave him his sisters in marriage. From these unions, he was gifted with two sons: Kalala Ilunga, son of Mabela, and Tshibinda Ilunga, son of Bulala.

Ilunga's fame continued to grow as the years passed. Eventually, this stirred jealousy in Kongolo's heart. Although Ilunga remained loyal, Kongolo could not sit still while his people praised Ilunga more than their king. Already forgetting the prophecy, Kongolo began plotting for Ilunga's assassination. However, the plan was foiled when his two sisters warned their husband in secret. Ilunga thanked them and took off his red feather and royal regalia. He then handed these tokens to his wives.

"Give these to our sons when they come of age," he instructed them. "Let them find me. I will recognize them as my own if they carry these signs."

That was the last time anyone ever saw Ilunga. It was as if he vanished out of thin air. However, this was not the end of his legacy. His sons would soon grow into formidable leaders. Kalala Ilunga would be the one to fulfil Mujibu's prophecy. Now a warrior, he returned to Kongolo's court and killed him, ending his tyrannical rule.

Kalala took the mantle and oversaw the flourishing of the Kingdom of Luba. Its power spread through ritual adoption (a practice in which local chiefs were symbolically incorporated into the royal family through sacred ceremonies), federations, and charisma. Chiefs from distant lands willingly aligned themselves with the sacred court in the capital, seeking to be part of a system that combined divine legitimacy with political strength. The king ruled from the capital, but he did not absorb the power of the local chiefs; they were allowed to retain control over their territories as long as they upheld their sacred obligations.

Central to the kingdom was also the Mbudye Society. This was a class of elite elders, seers, and memory-keepers. Their role seemed simple, yet the responsibility was immense. The Mbudye were the ones responsible for preserving the kingdom's most sacred assets, including the political traditions of the Luba people and the history of the kingdom. The Mbudye used lukasa, or memory boards. These hourglass-shaped wooden tablets were typically covered with beads and shells. While outsiders might see them as nothing more than just decoration, the people of Luba used lukasa to record their history. Not everyone could interpret the content of a lukasa. It could only be read by a diviner or a skilled historian. Instead of using eyes, the lukasa was read by running one's fingers across its surface.

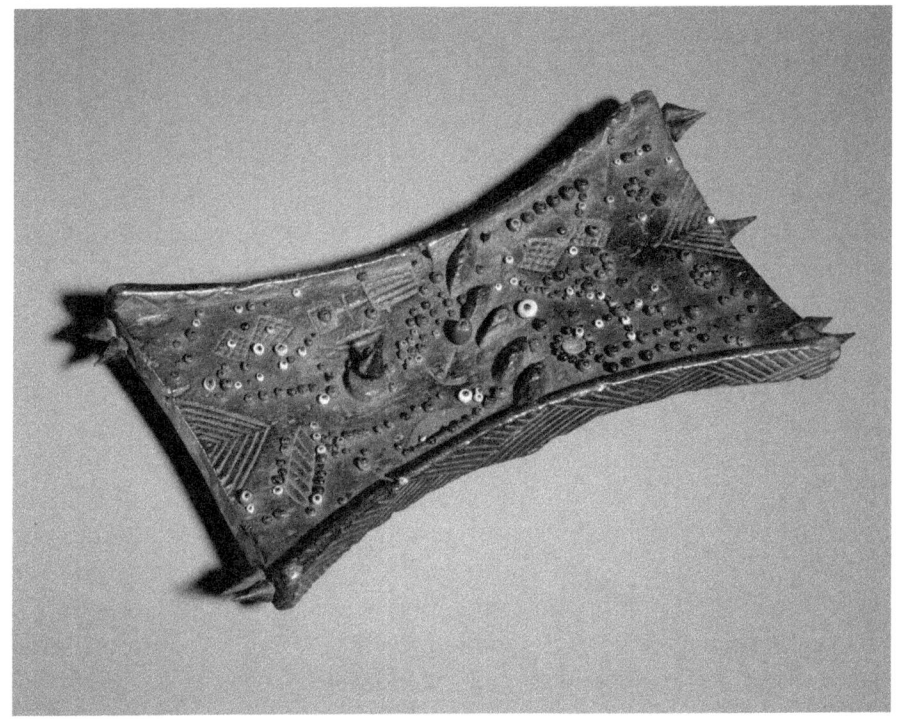

A lukasa memory board.[88]

It is safe to say that the Kingdom of Luba was strategically wealthy. Its lands were rich in natural resources. Copper was considered a valuable trade item and a symbol of spiritual power. Luba was known for producing iron tools and finely crafted raffia cloth, both of which were used as currency and tribute alongside salt gathered from inland basins. Luba traders were believed to have organized long-distance caravans that could reach into modern-day Zambia, Angola, and beyond, allowing them to exchange a variety of goods with neighboring polities. The kingdom's wealth was rarely displayed through grand palaces and colossal architecture. However, its wealth was evident in the strength of its networks, the abundance of its markets, and the quality of its artisan goods.

The kingdom enjoyed a period of expansion and stability throughout the 17th and early 18th centuries. It remained untouched by direct European interference for centuries. Things only began to change in the late 18th century when foreign traders and inland raiding groups like the Chokwe began showing their teeth. Armed by the Portuguese, the Chokwe made a move to press further into Luba lands.

This was only the beginning of the end. Luba prevailed until it entered a period of permanent decline following the arrival of the Belgians in 1885.

The Kingdom of Lunda

While Kalala ruled over Luba, another one of Ilunga's sons, Tshibinda, embarked on a journey westward. He crossed rivers, forests, and the savannah, eventually reaching the land of the Lunda people. At that time, the region was ruled by a queen named Lueji Naweej. The kingdom was young. It was still developing, and it was mostly held together by alliances and traditions.

Tshibinda married Queen Lueji. Legend has it that Lueji suffered from abnormal dysmenorrhea (menstrual cramps). She was often sick, making her unable to rule. So, she passed the responsibility solely to Tshibinda, who took the mantle as emperor. From here on, Tshibinda introduced the kingdom to the concepts of Mulopwe (sacred kingship), Mbudye-style councils, and ritual ceremonies that gave structure and legitimacy to the Lunda court. This was the beginning of the rise of the Lunda Empire. Under Tshibinda, the Lunda Empire grew tremendously, eventually rivalling or perhaps surpassing that of his brother.

Tshibinda's successors expanded the empire even more. The kingdom's central authority was based in Musumba. This royal capital was where the Mwaant Yaav (king of the kingdom) resided. Like the Luba Mulopwe, the Mwaant Yaav was believed to carry divine responsibility. However, unlike in Luba, the Lunda system was highly adaptable. Through ritual adoption and careful diplomacy, they created a network of allied states, where local rulers swore symbolic allegiance to Musumba while managing their own lands.

This system gave rise to a confederation of Lunda-linked states, each ruled by a local leader tied spiritually and ceremonially to the Mwaant

Yaav. At its height, Lunda's network of influence reached far into parts of present-day Angola, Zambia, and the southern Democratic Republic of Congo (DRC). Rulers of these states carried Lunda titles, wore Lunda symbols, and traced their legitimacy back to Musumba. Among these successor states were the Kazembe Kingdom and the Bemba chiefdoms, which would carry Lunda traditions well into the 19th century.

The Lunda were also great traders. They sat at the heart of several overland routes that connected the interior to both the Atlantic and Indian Ocean coasts. Lunda caravans typically carried copper, ivory, beeswax, and salt, linking Lunda territories to markets in Angola, the Congo River Basin, and eastern Central Africa. The wealth generated from this trade was more than enough to sustain the court and support large households of retainers, allowing the kingdom to project soft power far beyond its heartland.

However, a change was on the horizon when the world stepped into the 19th century. It was a change that the Lunda kings could not control. First came the Swahili and Arab merchants from the East African coast, who began reaching deep into the interior. They eventually succeeded in opening new trade routes that bypassed Musumba. With more options available, local chiefs began trading directly with these eastern networks. Over time, tribute to the Mwaant Yaav declined as these local rulers chose to keep the profits for themselves. Those who were bold enough declared themselves independent. Without the support of the local chiefs and their tributes, the Mwaant Yaav found himself in trouble.

The situation worsened even more after the death of a prominent Lunda ruler in the east, Kazembe VI. His death left a leadership vacuum that almost immediately resulted in an explosion of factional rivalries throughout the region. Disputes over succession, borders, and trade rights turned former allies against one another. The once well-organized confederation of Lunda-linked states fell deeper into disorder. Musumba remained a capital but only in name, as its influence was beyond repair.

Chapter 9 – The Hausa City-States: Urban Legends of Medieval West Africa

Long ago, in the land we now call northern Nigeria, was a well known as Kusugu (modern-day Daura). Legend has it that it was once a quiet place until the arrival of a snake known as Sarki. The creature did not wreak havoc by attacking the inhabitants blindly. Instead, the snake deprived them of water; Sarki remained near the well, guarding the town's only source of water. The inhabitants were only allowed to draw water from the well on Fridays.

The situation would change with the arrival of a stranger from the east. Some said his name was originally Abu Zaid and that he hailed from Baghdad, but the people of Kusugu called him Bayajidda. Despite being aware that Sarki was guarding the well, Bayajidda refused to heed the warning and went to fetch water on a Thursday. This enraged the monstrous snake. It attacked Bayajidda, but the stranger managed to evade its bite. Perhaps sensing an opening, he quickly unsheathed his sword and cut off the snake's head.

News of Sarki's death reached the people almost immediately. Bayajidda was invited to meet the queen of Kusugu.

"We are ever grateful for your action," Queen Daurama may have said to Bayajidda. "As a reward, I'm offering you half of my kingdom."

Bayajidda refused the reward, to the surprise of many. Instead of establishing a new kingdom himself, he asked for the queen's hand in marriage. The locals were shocked since their queens were known to have practiced celibacy. However, since Daurama felt indebted to Bayajidda, she accepted his proposal. From here on, Daura witnessed a major change in its political system. For years, it had been led by queens, but after Bayajidda, men wore the crown and ruled the land.

From this union, Bayajidda and Daurama had a son named Bawo. Many years later, Bawo fathered his own children; he had six sons in total. Interestingly, Bawo was not Bayajidda's only child. He also had another son named Biram through his earlier marriage with the daughter of the king of the Borno Empire (basically his first wife). Biram, together with Bawo's six sons, would grow to become the founders of the Hausa Kingdoms.

Collectively known as the Hausa Bakwai or the Seven True Hausa States, the kingdoms were named Biram, Daura, Kano, Katsina, Zaria (or Zazzau), Gobir, and Rano. These kingdoms shared similar origins, but each of them had its own story. Daura, the very place where the legend of Bayajidda and Sarki took place, was considered the spiritual heart of the Hausa Kingdoms. Kano and Katsina eventually flourished as trade centers with endless arrivals of merchants, craftsmen, and scholars. Zaria became known for its fierce warriors and, later, for its involvement in the trans-Saharan slave trade. Gobir grew into a formidable military stronghold, while Rano and Biram prospered somewhat quietly through farming and trade activities.

However, over time, seven more kingdoms rose in power close to the Hausa Bakwai. These later kingdoms adopted the Hausa language, customs, and political systems. Some suggest these kingdoms were established by the sons of Bayajidda and his concubine, while others claim they did not descend from Bayajidda's line at all. Regardless of their origins, it is safe to conclude that they were considered part of the same cultural world. They were known as the Banza Bakwai or "The Bastard Seven." Yes, the name may sound harsh, but in the context of the legend, it simply meant they stood outside the original bloodline. Despite the name, it is hard to dismiss that these states were far from insignificant; each of them was respected for its strength and trade influence.

The kingdoms included in the Banza Bakwai were Zamfara, Kebbi, Yauri, Nupe, Gwari, Kwararafa, and Ilorin. The relationship between these seven kingdoms and the Hausa Bakwai was complex, as they were both rivals and partners. Kebbi and Zamfara, for instance, constantly competed against the Hausa Bakwai for control over trade routes, farmland, and political influence. However, there were also times when they traded peacefully and shared cultural practices, especially through intermarriage and migration. Ilorin was initially a Yoruba town, but it became heavily Hausa-influenced after absorbing waves of migrants and religious influence. Nupe and Gwari, which were located farther south and neared the edge of forests, served as important links between the Hausa savannah and southern trade systems. Meanwhile, the confederation of Jukun-speaking peoples, Kwararafa, was best known for both its raids and diplomatic skills.

Administration and Power Behind the Walls

Despite being linked to each other—seven by blood and seven by culture—these fourteen Hausa city-states were never united under one crown or became a part of a single empire. Each was an independent kingdom, ruled by its own ruler. The rulers of the Hausa states were known formally as Sarkin Kasar, which means "king of the land." Also referred to simply as Sarki, these leaders were the ones expected to protect trade, settle disputes, command loyalty, and defend their city's honor, pretty much like any other king in history. The Sarki was viewed as both the chief executive and judge of the state. Typically, they ruled from their palaces, which were usually located at their city's center and protected by thick walls and gates. Kano, for one, was home to the Gidan Sarki, the best-preserved palace, where the king of Kano lived with his wives and children.

Of course, the Sarki of each state did not rule alone. He was backed by a council of advisors, which comprised respected nobles, Islamic judges, guild leaders, warriors, and sometimes influential women from royal households. True, the Sarki's words were final, but these advisors helped him shape decisions, manage conflicts, and ensure the smooth running of court life. Especially in city-states where Islam had taken a strong foothold, it was common for scholars and religious officials to play an even greater role; their advice and assistance often lent legitimacy to the king's rule through the language of faith and law.

It is safe to conclude that while the Hausa city-states were strong, there was not always peace. True, they shared the same origin story, culture, and language, but the city-states were often entangled in many episodes of rivalries and betrayals. It was common for ambition and jealousy to spark between them, igniting warfare and skirmishes. Take the fierce rivalry between Kano and Katsina as an example. Both city-states were located on key trade routes. Instead of simply sharing them, each state wished to dominate the flow of caravans carrying salt, cloth, and slaves. When one gained control of a trade corridor or a wealthy farming area, the other would retaliate. The 15th and 16th centuries saw both cities launching multiple military campaigns against each other. And these campaigns were not just small skirmishes. They were often large, involving the mobilization of entire armies.

Zamfara and Gobir frequently clashed with each other; their bitter wars were often the result of disputes over territory and grazing land. Their rivalry escalated in the 18th century when Gobir, which was located farther west, began showcasing its dominance over neighboring states. Over time, more raids were launched to claim tribute, cattle, and captives. Zamfara's discontent continued to grow, leading to fierce resistance. Wars were waged against the advancing Gobirawa, which unsurprisingly left villages in ashes and trade routes disrupted.

However, war was not the only answer to the disputes between these city-states. There were times when diplomacy was considered. Strategic marriages and hostage exchanges were two of the most common strategies for the kingdoms to forge peace and alliances. There were also times when their conflicts were settled by intervention by religious leaders who reminded rulers of their Islamic duty to avoid unnecessary bloodshed among fellow believers.

But still, these city-states were exceptional defenders. Each of them was surrounded by extensive defensive walls to protect the people from any danger. Kano's defensive walls (also called *ganuwa*) were some of the largest in Africa. Stretching over fourteen kilometers long, these walls protected not only the royal quarter but also the busy markets, mosques, and farmland. The gates were never left unattended. Guards stood their ground, their eyes always watching for even the smallest signs of trouble. Watchtowers were also constructed, allowing them to provide early warnings of attack.

The walls of Kano.[34]

These long defensive walls were not only built to hold off enemies from the neighboring kingdoms but also to deter threats from outsiders from beyond the continent. The mighty Songhai Empire, for instance, had its eyes on the Hausa region. When the world saw the rise of fearless Songhai rulers like Askia Muhammad, the Hausa region was left with no choice but to face serious threats from the empire, particularly in the late 15th and 16th centuries when the Songhai were aggressively expanding their borders. Katsina and Zamfara were two of the Hausa city-states that witnessed firsthand the military pressure laid by the Songhai. In the aftermath, they were forced to pay tribute to the invaders. Although the Songhai never succeeded in conquering the entire Hausa region, the threat was almost constant.

The Songhai were not the only ones attracted to the region. The Hausa also faced trouble from the Tuareg, the Teda, and the Bornu from the northeast. There were multiple episodes where the Hausa states resorted to unity to defend themselves. Some also allied with external powers to counter their enemies, but more often than not, these kinds of alliances were temporary. Some benefited from them, while others backfired, leading to betrayal or even partial occupation.

The Wealth of the Hausa City-States

While swords, defensive walls, and shifting alliances kept the Hausa city-states protected, trade was what made them thrive. Each city bustled with activity, its streets lined with open markets, artisans' workshops, and long lines of camels arriving from distant lands. Situated between the Sahara Desert to the north and the forest areas to the south, the Hausa Kingdoms became the middlemen in the flow of goods crossing West Africa.

Caravans from North Africa would come into these city-states, bringing heaps of salt, beads, fine cloth, and even horses that came from cities like Tripoli, Timbuktu, and Fez. Foreign merchants would then leave the Hausa city-states with an array of precious goods like kola nuts, gold, leather goods, dyed cloth, grain, and, of course, slaves. Trade in the cities was exceptionally organized. While local merchants, who typically belonged to powerful guilds, were responsible for regulating prices, maintaining standards, and protecting their members' interests, the city officials made sure that taxes were collected at the city gates. Soldiers also patrolled the trade routes, ensuring no bandits were bold enough to strike a caravan and leave with the goods.

Of the fourteen Hausa cities, Kano stood at the center of this commercial web. Its markets were considered among the largest in the region. It was a melting pot of traders from across the Sahel. It is also worth noting that Kano was more than just a trading hub. Back then, it was a city of craftsmen. Its most sought-after exports were leather goods. Many flocked to the city to get their hands on Kano's finely tanned leather bags, sandals, shields, and cushions. Its quality was made known to everyone, from those as far away as North Africa to even merchants from the Middle East.

Kano was also famous for its dyeing industry. The city was the home of the Kofar Mata dye pits, some of which are still used today. Here, the art of dyeing cloth was passed down through generations. The most popular dye was indigo, which was extracted from the *Indigofera* plant found growing in the region. The process began with the fermentation of the leaves of the *Indigofera* plant. This step took at least several days. Once fermentation was complete, the greenish liquid obtained from the leaves was then poured into clay-lined dye pits.

After this, the dyers would begin designing their creation. Cloth, usually cotton, was used as their canvas. The cloth was usually folded or tied into patterns and dipped into the pits; this was a method similar to tie-dye. Interestingly, when removed for the first time, the cloth would appear yellow-green. However, as it came into contact with air, the oxidation process transformed the fabric into a deep, rich blue.

Of course, this was not the end of the process. Each of these fabric pieces was not dyed just once. Many had to be dipped and aired repeatedly, sometimes up to twenty times, to achieve the best and darkest hues. The more dips, the more vibrant and durable the color. Afterward, the cloth was washed, dried under the sun, and prepared for sale or stitching.

Kofar Mata dye pits.[85]

Aside from this colorful side of the Hausa cities, the region also had a reputation for a darker trade: slavery. Zaria was one of the Hausa states that frequently launched raids into neighboring regions to obtain slaves. These raids were usually aimed at communities living south of the Hausa heartland, often in areas referred to by the Hausa as "pagan lands." The people there had not yet converted to Islam. They were seen as fair targets according to the customs of the time.

Raiding parties usually left during the dry season when travel was easier. Small and unfortified villages, as well as isolated farming communities, were their favorite targets. Scouts would usually leave the city first to gather intel before the rest of the raiding party came.

Their goal was simple enough. They were supposed to capture people, not kill them. Young men, women, and children were the most sought after, especially those who looked healthy and strong. Once captured, the victims were tied together with ropes or wooden yokes and marched north in long lines. Some of these unfortunate individuals ended up being sold in the markets of Zaria, Kano, or Katsina. Others were sent farther north toward Agadez and eventually across the Sahara into the larger networks of trans-Saharan slavery.

These slaves served different roles in the Hausa states. Some were put on the many farms to toil the land, tend horses, or build walls. Others worked in households or were sent to the barracks, where they were trained to serve in the military.

Life in the Hausa City-States

Before the region saw the arrival of Islam, the Hausa people held on to their traditional beliefs, which centered on nature, ancestors, and spirits—much like the majority of communities in the neighboring area. Shrines were typically erected near trees, rocks, or springs that the people believed to be sacred. They strongly believed in invisible forces, both good and dangerous, that influenced crops, health, and fortune. Priests and priestesses played a pivotal role in their faith. They acted as spiritual guides; they were the ones responsible for sacrifices and interpreting signs. In many areas, the king was thought to have divine protection, and his power was partly spiritual.

When Islam arrived, carried by Berber and Arab merchants from North Africa, things in the cities began to change. Rulers of cities like Kano, Katsina, and Zaria converted and began promoting Islamic learning, law, and values. Mosques soon dotted the city centers, and Qur'anic schools were established to teach children how to read Arabic and recite verses. Of course, not everything changed when Islam was made the official faith. In many cities, the faith blended with local beliefs. Spirits and charms continued to be part of daily life, and certain festivals kept their older meanings even after receiving Islamic names.

Most people in the Hausa cities lived in mud-walled compounds shared by extended families. They also featured courtyards, where children played and meals were prepared over open fires. Although most of the streets in the cities were rather narrow, they were never empty. With lines of small stalls, craftsmen's workshops, and wells, the streets were always busy. The markets were central to the people's everyday lives, but they were not strictly for trade or business. The markets were seen as social places. People came there to share news, arrange marriages, and resolve disputes.

Work, on the other hand, was structured around guilds. People of the same trade, like blacksmiths, weavers, butchers, or dyers, supported each other and upheld professional standards. It was common for children to learn their parents' trade from a young age. In Hausa cities, women also played a role in the economy. Some worked as potters or dyers, while others had their hands full processing food.

The Storm That Swept the Hausa States

The Hausa city-states were at their peak by the late 18th century. They were wealthy, proud, and deeply competitive. Trade was going smoothly, allowing wealth to flow into the royal coffers. Palaces expanded, and Islamic scholarship had taken root. However, wealth does not always mean peace. Problems brewed beneath the surface. Powerful kings began to impose heavy taxes on farmers and merchants. Court politics turned bitter. There were also issues with rulers who claimed to uphold Islamic values but lived in luxury. Justice became uneven. The local populations outside the palace, especially those in the countryside, began to voice their concerns. They were starting to feel the weight of a system that no longer served them.

Over time, these voices grew stronger. The boldest among them were the Fulani. These semi-nomadic people had lived among the Hausa but still maintained their own identity. The majority of them were devout Muslims who believed that the version of Islam practiced in the cities was becoming more corrupt each day. In their eyes, the faith practiced in the cities had mixed too much with old traditions. It was too lenient and too focused on wealth. The Fulani could no longer sit still and watch as the Hausa leaders appointed unqualified judges and neglected the charitable tax known as zakat. They were also infuriated by how the leaders tolerated rituals that blended Islamic prayers with ancestral spirit worship. To the Fulani, this was not true Islam but a hollow performance used to justify power.

In Gobir, a certain Fulani scholar and preacher began to draw attention. Known as Usman dan Fodio, he considered himself a reformer. He called for a return to pure Islam, the end of oppression, and the need for rulers who ruled by faith and fairness. Many poor Hausa villagers shared his frustrations. The king of Gobir tried to silence him, but he failed. Instead, it sparked a rebellion that would grow far beyond anyone's expectations.

Things went south for the Hausa rulers when Usman dan Fodio declared a jihad (a holy war) against them in 1804. The next few years saw his followers, referred to as the Jama'a, march relentlessly from one village to another to gather support. This was not merely a rebellion of commoners. Many Hausa states eventually fell, including Gobir, Kano, Katsina, and Zaria. Some were defeated in a clash of swords, while others chose to surrender, avoiding major conflicts and unnecessary destruction. Some rulers fled for their lives. Those who were headstrong enough to stand their ground were killed.

The fall of the Hausa Kingdoms gave way to the emergence of the Sokoto Caliphate.

Chapter 10 – Women of Medieval Africa: An Overlooked Legacy

There was a time when the Kingdom of Aksum ruled proudly over the highlands of East Africa. Its stone obelisks could be seen piercing the sky, and its ships constantly sailed the Red Sea, reaching as far as the shores of Arabia, the Roman world, and even India. The kingdom rose to power in the 1st century CE. It reached its height sometime between the 4th and 7th centuries, largely due to the kingdom's ability to control the trade routes across the Horn of Africa.

The obelisks of Aksum.[86]

However, despite being known for its significant trade achievements, the Aksumite kings were not mere traders. They were also pioneers of the Christian faith. It all began in the year 330 CE when King Ezana made a decision that shocked many; he converted to Christianity. Aksum became one of the first Christian kingdoms in the world, even before much of Europe. The cross became a royal symbol of the Aksumite kings. Stone churches began to dot the kingdom, and the sight of priests in white robes became increasingly common.

Aksum succeeded in expanding its wings across the continent. Its power could be felt in parts of modern-day Ethiopia, Eritrea, Sudan, and even southern Arabia. However, nothing is meant to last forever, and the same could be said of the mighty Aksumite Kingdom. It began to see a few glimpses of its decline by the 8th and 9th centuries. There was not a single reason that contributed to its decline; it was driven by a combination of many factors. First, there were the shifting trade routes that followed the rise of Islamic ports along the Red Sea. Climate change might have also affected local farming. Scholars and historians also point their fingers at internal conflicts and religious tensions.

Map detailing the territories under the Aksumite Kingdom.[87]

Being a kingdom that once held so much power, it was not surprising that many were waiting in the shadows for an opportunity to arise, one that could bury the kingdom once and for all. One of them was a female ruler who went by the name Gudit.

Some Ethiopian accounts called her Yodit. Though her name rarely appeared in written sources, her story is often remembered through oral traditions. Her origin and background, however, remain a debate. While some suggest she was a Jewish queen whose roots could be traced back to the communities that had long resisted Christian rule, others claimed she came from a Cushitic-speaking pagan group in the south or southeast of the Aksumite heartland. There are also a few narratives that describe her as part of the Beta Israel (the Ethiopian Jewish community known for practicing a form of Judaism rooted in the Hebrew Bible).

It is important to note that the stories about Yodit are often semi-legendary. More often than not, they were shaped more by memory and fear rather than official record. Descriptions of her vary depending on the version of the story, but one detail is constant: Yodit was an outsider. She did not rise from within the Aksumite court, and she was far from an ordinary queen who ruled quietly from her throne.

It is uncertain why Yodit chose to attack Aksum. Many believe it was a mix of religious rejection, political ambition, and possible revenge. If she belonged to a non-Christian or marginalized community, she might have seen Aksum's rulers as symbols of exclusion or oppression. According to some oral traditions, her campaign was an act of retaliation after years of suffering under Christian rule. It is also plausible that she attacked the kingdom simply because she saw an opportunity when Aksum was declining.

Regardless of the reason, her campaign was relentless. It was as if she were not content with only raiding and rebelling. She also came to erase. Yodit received massive support from the discontented groups in southern or eastern Ethiopia. These were the people who had been excluded from Aksumite rule. Therefore, Yodit was seen as a liberator.

Yodit led her people across the northern highlands, wreaking havoc. Churches were burned, and monasteries were destroyed. Those who dared to stand their ground met her sword. Some accounts claim she marched into Aksum itself, where she destroyed sacred sites and ended the line of kings that had ruled for centuries. Another version narrated how she established her own dynasty, ruling for forty years before eventually passing the crown to her descendants.

In the eyes of many Ethiopian monks and court scribes, Yodit was remembered as a figure of terror and havoc. Her ruthless campaign brought about a long period of fragmentation in the Ethiopian Highlands. Others, however, saw her as a visionary who managed to seize power in a world that had long denied it to women and outsiders. So, was she a villain or simply an ambitious person? Perhaps her story was more complicated than it seems, and her character lies somewhere in between.

African Women in the Medieval World

Across most of the medieval world, it was rare for women to possess real power—be it in governance, business, or even their own households. In Europe, for example, noblewomen were usually confined to castles and convents. Men made sure women's influence was limited to family alliances and, at times, inheritance. On the other side of the world, particularly in China, women were often bound by marriage and expected to meet certain beauty ideals. They were typically kept out of public life by Confucian laws. The Islamic world was not much different. While there were instances when women had power during the early years of the faith, things changed. As they stepped into the medieval era, Muslim women found themselves largely removed from the political stage.

However, in many parts of Africa, the situation was different. In contrast to kingdoms and empires on other continents, women in medieval Africa held real and visible power. From the savannah kingdoms of West Africa to the Christian courts of Nubia to the coastal cities of Swahili, there are stories of women owning their own land, leading armies, advising kings, and even becoming monarchs. The latter could be seen in African societies that followed matrilineal traditions, where lineage and political legitimacy were traced through the mother's line. Through this system, a king might be crowned not because of his father but because of his connection to a royal woman like his mother, grandmother, or aunt. It is clear that this system heightened the standard of women. Queen mothers and female elders played key roles in not just diplomacy but also governance and succession.

Even in Islamic states and kingdoms that practiced patrilineal traditions, African women were still allowed to carve out space for themselves. States like Mali and Songhai allowed women to manage their own wealth and trade. The same could be said about the cities on the Swahili coast, where women played a major role in commerce and property ownership.

Meanwhile, in Christian Nubia, the discovery of inscriptions and burial records proved that most of the elite women held titles. Their deeds were never erased. Most of them donated to churches and occasionally governed as regents. Yes, the number of female rulers was fewer than their male counterparts. However, the numbers alone do not define the power they once had. In the history of medieval Africa, several female figures stepped into the role of leader, especially during times of war or dynastic crisis.

Some may ask what made this possible. Part of the answer lies in the very nature of African societies. Many kingdoms and city-states on the continent were built on networks of kinship and alliance. Mothers, sisters, and daughters mattered as much as kings and warriors. Almost all of the African societies held strong to oral tradition, which kept the memory of powerful women alive, even when written history tried to erase them. And of course, in a world where survival also depended on adaptability, it was hard for them to completely ignore and dismiss women who clearly showed strength and wisdom.

Queen Dihya, the Desert Warrior Who Resisted the Arabs Until Her Last Breath

The Arab armies were confident they would soon return to their homeland, bringing news of victory. They had already conquered Egypt and captured the Byzantine city of Carthage. They wasted no time in pushing westward into the Maghreb, hoping they could bring more territories under Umayyad control. However, before they could reach the Atlantic, they would meet their match in the rugged mountains of North Africa. They had entered the home of the Berbers, who were known to be fiercely independent and deeply rooted in their traditions. Like the Arabs, the Berbers, also known as the Amazigh, were no strangers to war. Interestingly, the Arab forces would not clash against armies led by men. Instead, they were led by a powerful woman named Queen Dihya.

A 19th century painting of Queen Dihya or al-Kahina.[88]

Dihya rose to prominence in the 7th century, a time that saw the early wave of Arab-Islamic expansion campaigns. With Muslim generals marching westward, bringing with them both a new faith and a new rule, the local tribes found themselves at a crossroads. They could surrender peacefully, but they would be forced to abandon their ancient beliefs and traditions as they faced conversion. Or they could resist and fight until the last drop of blood. Dihya chose to resist.

The Berber queen's origins traced back to the Aurès Mountains in what is now eastern Algeria. This region was known for its fierce fighters and highland fortresses. According to oral traditions, Dihya was a military leader and a prophetess. Even her Arabic name, al-Kahina, is translated to "the seer" or "the priestess." Accounts of her belief vary, though. While many suggested she was a follower of the traditional Amazigh religion, others claimed she was Jewish. There are a few Islamic sources that suggest she followed elements of Christian beliefs. Regardless of this uncertainty, one detail about the queen remained constant across all narratives: she was an impressive leader.

Dihya succeeded in uniting a broad coalition of Berber tribes, especially those who had grown extremely restless following the arrival of the Arab forces. Resistance efforts were common during this time, but many were quickly crushed by the invading forces. This did not deter Dihya. The queen eventually met the Arabs under the command of Hasan ibn al-Nu'man near Meskiana (in modern-day Algeria). Hasan had heard about Dihya being one of the most powerful monarchs in the region. He knew that if Dihya was defeated, he would receive submission from the rest of the Berber tribes in no time.

Things immediately went south for the Arabs when Dihya and her Berber forces launched their attack on the battlefield. Her sound victory forced the Arabs to retreat to Libya. Hasan remained in this region for nearly five years while planning his next move. Dihya knew that this would not be the Arabs' last attempt to seize control of the region. Therefore, she took a drastic step. She ordered a scorched-earth campaign, destroying towns, wells, farmlands, and anything that could support the enemy. This campaign did not heavily impact the mountain and desert tribes, but it did not sit well with the sedentary oasis-dwellers. When the Arabs returned years later, with Hasan at the forefront once more, some of her own turned against her.

Dihya and her Berber forces clashed with the Arabs again at the Battle of Tabarka, which took place possibly in 703 CE. Unfortunately, this was the end of the line for the powerful queen. Dihya was said to have died in the battle, sword in hand. However, there are other accounts that suggest she committed suicide, choosing death rather than submitting to the enemy. Her head was decapitated and sent to the Umayyad caliph in Damascus as proof of her death.

Despite her death, Dihya's name continues to be remembered. To the Berbers, she became a symbol of resistance, independence, and pride. Later, she was used as a symbol against male hegemony and, much later, during the French colonization of Algeria, Dihya became a model for the militant women who fought the French.

Fatima al-Fihriya

While women like Yodit and Dihya have their names immortalized for military might, many shaped their stories in quieter ways. Some made their name through counsel, others through ritual leadership, education, and trade. It is important to note that power in medieval Africa was not always tied to the sword. Fatima al-Fihriya, for one, had her name remembered neither on the ruins of a palace nor the battlefield but rather in the walls of a university that still stands proudly today.

Her story began in the 9th century in the growing city of Fez in northern Morocco. Fatima was not originally from Fez. Her family had migrated there from Kairouan (in modern-day Tunisia). They were part of a wave of Arab settlers in North Africa following the expansion of Islam. Not much is known about her early life, but it is safe to assume that Fatima's life was not daunting. Her father, Muhammad al-Fihri al-Qayrawanni, was a successful Quraysh merchant. However, tragedy soon struck, as Fatima lost her father, brother, and husband within a short time. Because of these deaths, Fatima and her sister Mariam inherited a significant fortune. However, instead of keeping the wealth for themselves or perhaps using it to leverage their position, the sisters chose to invest in charity.

While her sister commissioned the al-Andalus Mosque, Fatima built the al-Qarawiyyin Mosque, which had an impressive architectural design. With her wealth, Fatima was able to employ the most skilled engineers and craftsmen and used materials of the highest quality. Staying true to the classical Islamic architectural layout for a mosque complex, the al-Qarawiyyin Mosque featured a large ceramic-tiled courtyard. Here, visitors could find a fountain basin, which was used by worshipers to perform their ablutions before prayer. The courtyard was surrounded by shaded walkways, which led to the large prayer hall. One could also find a library in the mosque complex. Of course, the mosque had a tall minaret where the call to prayer was made by a *muezzin*.

The entrance to the prayer hall.[39]

The University of al-Qarawiyyin today.[40]

The mosque was founded in 859 CE, and it was located in the heart of Fez. As a religious complex, it was a place where scholars, worshipers, and students from across the Islamic world would converge. However, over time, it expanded. From a mosque, it grew into the University of al-Qarawiyyin. One of the oldest universities in the world, it featured classrooms, libraries, and dormitories. Here, students were taught a range of subjects, from Islamic law and theology to astronomy, mathematics, medicine, and even grammar. Over time, students from beyond the continent flocked to the university. Some hailed from Iraq, while others came all the way from Spain. Even famous thinkers like Ibn Khaldun and Averroes (ibn Rushd) were said to have visited the university and passed through its halls.

A document written in Arabic stored in the library at al-Qarawiyyin. Issued in 1207, the document is believed to be the world's oldest surviving medical degree.[ii]

Fatima is remembered as a pious and visionary woman. She fasted throughout the long months of construction and oversaw the building with care and devotion. While records about her personal life are limited, her act of founding the university speaks volumes. In a time when most educational institutions were founded and controlled by men, Fatima succeeded in creating a place where knowledge and faith met. Most importantly, it became a center where generations, no matter their gender, could learn and teach.

Fatima passed away in 880 CE, but her legacy still stands. The University of al-Qarawiyyin still operates to this day and has been recognized by UNESCO and the Guinness World Records as the oldest existing and continuously operating degree-granting university in the world.

Conclusion

Suffice it to say that the story of medieval Africa is complex. It does not revolve only around kings, crowns, gold, and trade. Through these pages, we have seen it was an era of transformation. It was a time when empires rose, declined, and replaced others. It was an era when African cities flourished, attracting the attention of outsiders as far as Asia. This was not a period of peace or chaos. Throughout the pages, we have seen borders shift, cities grow and be destroyed, faiths compete, cultures collide and merge, and new ideas pass along dusty roads and coastal harbors.

This journey through medieval Africa is not about telling a separate story. It is about placing Africa back inside the world's story, where it has always belonged. When we think of the Middle Ages, we should not only imagine scenes of knights in shining armor and Gothic castles that took centuries to complete or even the emperors of China and the samurai of Japan. We should also recall the story of how Mansa Musa carried the Mali Empire to its height of power, of Queen Dihya who resisted the Arab forces until she breathed her last, of Fatima al-Fihriya who chose to use her wealth for the improvement of education, of the Saifawa dynasty who brought the Kanem-Bornu Empire closer to the Ottoman Empire, and of the many Hausa city-states that were once bustling centers of trade, scholarship, and military power.

This book is not the end of African history. Rather, we end at the start of yet another chapter. Colonialism would soon arrive on the continent, and its arrival ushered in a new kind of struggle. Despite the arrival of these more advanced and modern societies, the strength, brilliance, and complexity of the Africans did not vanish. The people adapted, resisted, and endured, sometimes openly and sometimes in silence.

To preserve this history is not only about honoring the past but also about restoring a truth that was altered or nearly erased. These are the kinds of stories that remind us and future generations that Africa was never on the edge of the medieval world. These voices and legacies deserve to be remembered, studied, and passed on. Only when we see Africa clearly can we begin to see world history more truthfully.

Here's another book by Matt Clayton that you might like

Free Bonus from Captivating History (Available for a Limited time)

Hi History Lovers!

Now you have a chance to join our exclusive history list so you can get your first history ebook for free as well as discounts and a potential to get more history books for free!

Simply visit the link below to join.

Or, Scan the QR code!

captivatinghistory.com/ebook

Also, make sure to follow us on Facebook, X, and YouTube by searching for Captivating History.

Bibliography

"5 Centuries in Business: Nigeria's Ancient Dye Pits." *Daily Sabah*, 19 Jan. 2021, www.dailysabah.com/gallery/5-centuries-in-business-nigerias-ancient-dye-pits/images.

Ahmed, Sikeena Karmali. "Fatima Al-Fihri and Al-Qarawiyyin University." *World History*, 7 Mar. 2025, www.worldhistory.org/article/2662/fatima-al-fihri-and-al-qarawiyyin-university.

"The Almohad Empire." *Think Africa*, 27 Feb. 2021, thinkafrica.net/thealmohadempire.

"The Almoravid Dynasty." *Think Africa*, 28 Feb. 2021, thinkafrica.net/thealmoraviddynasty.

"The Ancient Remains of Great Zimbabwe." *BBC*, 26 Sept. 2022, www.bbc.com/travel/article/20220925-the-ancient-remains-of-great-zimbabwe.

"Atlantic Worlds: Enslavement and Resistance." *Royal Museums Greenwich*, www.rmg.co.uk/stories/topics/history-transatlantic-slave-trade. Accessed 2 May 2025.

"Bayajidda: The legend of Hausa land." *DW*, 26 Jan. 2018, www.dw.com/en/Bayajidda-the-legend-of-hausa-land/a-42291985.

"Berber Queen Dihya." *AFA*, www.afa-afa.org/african-queens/berber-queen-dihyaibn-khaldn-of-algeria. Accessed 28 Apr. 2025.

Beyer, Greg. "Songhai Empire: The Rise and Fall of Africa's Biggest Empire." *The Collector*, 24 Nov. 2023, www.thecollector.com/songhai-empire-africa.

Bilow, Ali. "Empire of Kanem-Bornu (Ca. 9th Century-1900)." *Blackpast*, 29 Dec. 2008, www.blackpast.org/global-african-history/places-global-african-history/empire-kanem-bornu-c-9th-century-1900.

Boddy-Evans, Alistair. "Biography of Sonni Ali, Songhai Monarch." *ThoughtCo*, 13 June 2019, www.thoughtco.com/biography-sonni-ali-44234.

Cartwright, Mark. "Hausaland." *World History*, 9 May 2019, www.worldhistory.org/Hausaland.

Cartwright, Mark. "Ghana Empire." *World History*, 5 Mar. 2019, www.worldhistory.org/Ghana_Empire.

Cartwright, Mark. "Kingdom of Kanem." *World History*, 23 Apr. 2019, www.worldhistory.org/timeline/Kingdom_of_Kanem.

Cartwright, Mark. "Kingdom of Luba." *World History*, 1 Apr. 2020, www.worldhistory.org/Kingdom_of_Luba.

Cartwright, Mark. "Songhai Empire." *World History*, 8 Mar. 2019, www.worldhistory.org/Songhai_Empire.

Chaplow, Chris, and Fiona Flores Watson. "The Battle of Las Navas De Tolosa." *Andalucia.com*, www.andalucia.com/spainsmoorishhistory/las-navas-de-tolosa.htm. Accessed 18 Apr. 2025.

Conliffe, Ciaran. "The Ajuran Empire." *Daily Scribbling*, dailyscribbling.com/forgotten-empires/the-ajuran-empire. Accessed 23 Apr. 2025.

Dimri, Bipin. "The Battle of Guadalete: How Islam Fought Its Way Into Spain." *Historic Mysteries*, 7 Oct. 2022, www.historicmysteries.com/history/battle-of-guadalete/27814.

Espley, Simon. "Thulamela Ancient Kruger Walled Kingdom." *Africa Geographic*, 20 Jan. 2021, africageographic.com/stories/thulamela.

"Great Zimbabwe." *National Geographic*, 19 Oct. 2023, https://education.nationalgeographic.org/resource/great-zimbabwe/

"History of the Lost Civilization of Mapungubwe." *Siyabona Africa*, www.nature-reserve.co.za/lost-civilization-mapungubwe-history.html. Accessed 20 Apr. 2025.

"Husuni Kubwa Palace, Kilwa, Tanzania - Reconstruction." *World History*, 14 May 2021, www.worldhistory.org/image/14025/husuni-kubwa-palace-kilwa-tanzania---reconstructio.

"The Kingdom of Luba." *Sankayi*, sankayi.com/the-origins-of-the-luba-kingdom. Accessed 30 Apr. 2025.

"The Kongo Kingdom." *Africa Museum*, www.africamuseum.be/en/discover/history_articles/kongo-kingdom. Accessed 30 Apr. 2025.

"The Legend of Alfarouk." *Timbuktu-lopac*, https://timbuktu-lopac.tumblr.com/post/129063751661/the-legend-of-alfarouk. Accessed 8 Apr. 2025.

"The Mali Kingdom And Mansa Musa Were Imperialist Slave Traders." *Balanta*, 3 Feb. 2020, www.balanta.org/history/the-mali-kingdom-was-imperialist-revisiting-african-history-from-the-point-of-view-of-the-people-who-were-oppressed.

Mitchell, Robbie. "The Kilwa Sultanate: The Island State That Dominated Medieval East Africa." *Ancient Origins*, 16 May 2023, www.ancient-origins.net/ancient-places-africa/kilwa-sultanate-0018457.

Mohamud, Naima. "Is Mansa Musa the Richest Man Who Ever Lived?" *BBC*, 10 Mar. 2019, www.bbc.com/news/world-africa-47379458.

"Portuguese Intervention in the West." *BBC*, www.bbc.co.uk/worldservice/africa/features/storyofafrica/10chapter4.shtml. Accessed 20 Apr. 2025.

Samuel, Isaac. "Centralizing Power in an African Pastoral Society: The Ajuran Empire of Somalia (16th-17th Century)." *African History Extra*, 17 July 2022, www.africanhistoryextra.com/p/centralizing-power-in-an-african.

Stephen, Olubayo. "Rain Makers in Africa: The Art and Practice of Controlling the Elements." *Oriole*, 8 May 2023, www.oriire.com/article/rain-makers-in-africa-the-art-and-practice-of-controlling-the-elements.

"Sundiata Keita." *National Geographic*, https://education.nationalgeographic.org/resource/sundiata-keita/. Accessed 8 Apr. 2025.

Image Sources

1 Aa77zz, CC0, via Wikimedia Commons:
   https://commons.wikimedia.org/wiki/File:Trans-Saharan_routes_early.svg

2 Holger Reineccius, CC BY-SA 3.0 <http://creativecommons.org/licenses/by-sa/3.0/>, via Wikimedia Commons:
   https://commons.wikimedia.org/wiki/File:Bilma-Salzkarawane1.jpg

3 https://commons.wikimedia.org/wiki/File:Malicavalry.jpg

4 https://commons.wikimedia.org/wiki/File:Catalan_Atlas_BNF_Sheet_6_
   Mansa_Musa_(cropped).jpg

5 Gabriel Moss, CC BY-SA 4.0 <https://creativecommons.org/licenses/by-sa/4.0>, via
   Wikimedia Commons: https://commons.wikimedia.org/wiki/
   File:The_Mali_Empire.jpg

6 KaTeznik, CC BY-SA 2.0 FR <https://creativecommons.org/licenses/by-sa/2.0/fr/deed.en>, via Wikimedia Commons:
   https://commons.wikimedia.org/wiki/File:Djingareiber_cour.jpg

7 https://commons.wikimedia.org/wiki/File:Fortier_368_Timbuktu_Sankore
   _Mosque.jpg

8 Holger Reineccius, CC BY-SA 2.0 DE <https://creativecommons.org/licenses/by-sa/2.0/de/deed.en>, via Wikimedia Commons:
   https://commons.wikimedia.org/wiki/File:Djado-nah.jpg

9 https://commons.wikimedia.org/wiki/File:Group_of_Kanem-Bu_warriors.jpg

10 https://commons.wikimedia.org/wiki/File:Bodyguard_of_the_Sheikh_of_
   Bornu,_early_1820%27s.jpg

11 Ermanarich, CC BY-SA 4.0 <https://creativecommons.org/licenses/by-sa/4.0>, via
   Wikimedia Commons: https://commons.wikimedia.org/wiki/File:Kanem-
   Bornu_1650.svg

12 HetmanTheResearcher, CC BY-SA 4.0 <https://creativecommons.org/licenses/by-sa/4.0>, via Wikimedia Commons: https://commons.wikimedia.org/wiki/File:Map_of_the_Songhay_Empire.png

13 https://commons.wikimedia.org/wiki/File:Timbuktu-manuscripts-astronomy-mathematics.jpg

14 Taguelmoust, CC BY-SA 3.0 <http://creativecommons.org/licenses/by-sa/3.0/>, via Wikimedia Commons: https://commons.wikimedia.org/wiki/File:Askia.jpg

15 https://commons.wikimedia.org/wiki/File:Great-Zimbabwe-3.jpg

16 Janice Bell, CC BY-SA 4.0 <https://creativecommons.org/licenses/by-sa/4.0>, via Wikimedia Commons: https://commons.wikimedia.org/wiki/File:Great-zim-aerial-looking-West,JPG

17 Marius Loots, CC BY-SA 3.0 <https://creativecommons.org/licenses/by-sa/3.0>, via Wikimedia Commons: https://commons.wikimedia.org/wiki/File:Conical_tower.jpg

18 J. Patrick Fischer, CC BY 3.0 <https://creativecommons.org/licenses/by/3.0>, via Wikimedia Commons: https://commons.wikimedia.org/wiki/File:Zim-bird.jpg

19 https://commons.wikimedia.org/wiki/File:Flag_of_Zimbabwe.svg

20 South African Tourism from South Africa, CC BY 2.0 <https://creativecommons.org/licenses/by/2.0>, via Wikimedia Commons: https://commons.wikimedia.org/wiki/File:Mapungubwe,_Limpopo,_South_Africa_(20356187550).jpg)

21 Vassia Atanassova - Spiritia, CC BY-SA 4.0 <https://creativecommons.org/licenses/by-sa/4.0>, via Wikimedia Commons: https://commons.wikimedia.org/wiki/File:Mapungubwe_gold_beads_and_jewellery_-_Museum_of_Gems_and_Jewellery.jpg

22 https://commons.wikimedia.org/wiki/File:The_battle_of_Guadelete.jpg

23 BRAHIM DJELLOUL Mustapha, CC BY-SA 4.0 <https://creativecommons.org/licenses/by-sa/4.0>, via Wikimedia Commons: https://commons.wikimedia.org/wiki/File:Grande_mosqu%C3%A9e_et_d%C3%A9pendance_Minaret_de_la_Mosqu%C3%A9e_003.jpg

24 Flaspec, CC BY-SA 4.0 <https://creativecommons.org/licenses/by-sa/4.0>, via Wikimedia Commons: https://commons.wikimedia.org/wiki/File:Almohad_dynasty_of_Morocco-en.svg

25 https://commons.wikimedia.org/wiki/File:Batalla_de_las_Navas_de_Tolosa,_por_Francisco_van_Halen.jpg

26 https://commons.wikimedia.org/wiki/File:Stamp_Aden_1937_0.5a.jpg

27 https://commons.wikimedia.org/wiki/File:City_of_Kilwa,_1572.jpg

28 CosMapi, CC BY-SA 4.0 <https://creativecommons.org/licenses/by-sa/4.0>, via Wikimedia Commons: https://commons.wikimedia.org/wiki/File:Kilwa-Kisiwani-ruins-tanzania.jpg

29 Khalidsalewa, CC BY-SA 4.0 <https://creativecommons.org/licenses/by-sa/4.0>, via Wikimedia Commons: https://commons.wikimedia.org/wiki/File: Great_Mosque_Kilwa_Interior.jpg

30 Scoobycentric, CC BY-SA 3.0 <https://creativecommons.org/licenses/by-sa/3.0>, via Wikimedia Commons: https://commons.wikimedia.org/wiki/ File:Marka,Somalia.jpg

31 Ms. Milora Lipscomb, Mr. Bruce Mateso and Paari-editeur, CC BY-SA 2.5 <https://creativecommons.org/licenses/by-sa/2.5>, via Wikimedia Commons: https://commons.wikimedia.org/wiki/File:Lukeni_Lua_Nimi-2_(1)_(1).jpg

32 https://commons.wikimedia.org/wiki/File:The_Baptism_of_Jo%C3%A3o_ I_Nzinga_a_Nkuwu_(King_of_Kongo).jpg

33 Brooklyn Museum, CC BY 3.0 <https://creativecommons.org/licenses/by/3.0>, via Wikimedia Commons: https://commons.wikimedia.org/wiki/File: Brooklyn_Museum_76.20.4_Lukasa_Memory_Board.jpg

34 Cepit, CC BY-SA 4.0 <https://creativecommons.org/licenses/by-sa/4.0>, via Wikimedia Commons: https://commons.wikimedia.org/wiki/File:Kano_Wall_1.jpg

35 Solasly, CC BY-SA 4.0 <https://creativecommons.org/licenses/by-sa/4.0>, via Wikimedia Commons: https://commons.wikimedia.org/ wiki/File:Kofar_Matar_Dye_Pit,_Kano.jpg

36 Tesfawel, CC BY-SA 4.0 <https://creativecommons.org/licenses/by-sa/4.0>, via Wikimedia Commons: https://commons.wikimedia.org/wiki/File: Aksum_obelisk.jpg

37 Newslea Staff, CC BY-SA 4.0 <https://creativecommons.org/licenses/by-sa/4.0>, via Wikimedia Commons: https://commons.wikimedia.org/wiki/File: Kingdom_of_Aksum_Map.png

38 https://commons.wikimedia.org/wiki/File:Dihya_Berber_ Queen_of_the_Aur%C3%A8s_by_Vernet-Lecomte.jpg

39 Anderson sady, CC BY-SA 3.0 <https://creativecommons.org/licenses/by-sa/3.0>, via Wikimedia Commons: https://commons.wikimedia.org/wiki/File:Al-Karaouine_University_(Al-Qarawiyyin)_in_the_city_of_Fes,_Morocco_(Image_8_of_9).jpg

40 R Prazeres, CC BY-SA 4.0 <https://creativecommons.org/licenses/by-sa/4.0>, via Wikimedia Commons: https://commons.wikimedia.org/wiki/File:Qarawiyyin_Mosque_DSCF4250.jpg

41 https://commons.wikimedia.org/wiki/File:Oldest_known_and_documented_ MD_degree_delivered_in_the_world.png

www.ingramcontent.com/pod-product-compliance
Lightning Source LLC
Chambersburg PA
CBHW071521120626
46550CB00006B/2307